'04   10·19·19   2.00

D0961353

ALSO BY MAX FRANKEL

The Times of My Life and My Life with The Times

HIGH NOON IN THE COLD WAR

HIGH NOON
IN THE
COLD WAR

Kennedy, Khrushchev,
and the Cuban Missile Crisis

MAX FRANKEL

BALLANTINE BOOKS

NEW YORK

A Presidio Press Book
Published by The Random House Publishing Group

Copyright © 2004 by Max Frankel

All rights reserved under International and Pan-American
Copyright Conventions. Published in the United States by Ballantine Books,
an imprint of The Random House Publishing Group, a division of
Random House, Inc., New York, and simultaneously in Canada by
Random House of Canada Limited, Toronto.

Owing to limitations of space, permissions acknowledgments can be found on p. 185,
which constitutes an extension of this copyright page.

Presidio Press and colophon are trademarks of Random House, Inc.

www.presidiopress.com

LIBRARY OF CONGRESS CATALOGING-IN-PUBLICATION DATA
Frankel, Max, 1930–
High noon in the Cold War: Kennedy, Khrushchev, and the Cuban missile crisis /
Max Frankel.
p.   cm.
Includes bibliographical references and index.
ISBN 0-345-46505-9
1. Cuban Missile Crisis, 1962.   2. Kennedy, John F. (John Fitzgerald), 1917–1963.
3. Khrushchev, Nikita Sergeevich, 1894–1971.   4. United States—Foreign relations—
Soviet Union.   5. Soviet Union—Foreign relations—United States. I. Title.
E841.F68 2004   327.47073'09'046—dc22   2004046159

ISBN 0-345-46505-9

Map illustration by Max Frankel

Manufactured in the United States of America

First Edition: October 2004

2 4 6 8 9 7 5 3 1

Book design by Casey Hampton

FOR JOYCE

*With the hope that saner times will prevail in the lives of
Jen & David, Margot & Joel, Erin & Jon,
Julia, Asher, Phoebe & Jake.*

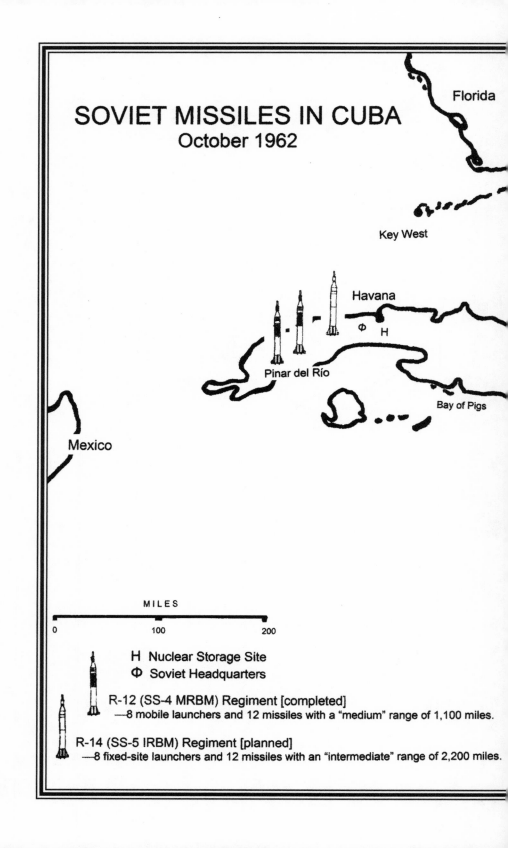

SOVIET MISSILES IN CUBA
October 1962

Florida

Key West

Havana
Φ H

Pinar del Río

Bay of Pigs

Mexico

MILES

0   100   200

H Nuclear Storage Site
Φ Soviet Headquarters

R-12 (SS-4 MRBM) Regiment [completed]
——8 mobile launchers and 12 missiles with a "medium" range of 1,100 miles.

R-14 (SS-5 IRBM) Regiment [planned]
——8 fixed-site launchers and 12 missiles with an "intermediate" range of 2,200 miles.

ami

The Bahamas

CUBA

Banes

Sierra Maestra   Guantánamo

Haiti

Jamaica

CONTENTS

AUTHOR'S NOTE

Histories of the Cuban Missile Crisis have appeared in every decade since October 1962, and they have progressively uncovered more secrets and memories not only in the United States but also, at last, in Russia and Cuba. The revelations and ever more informed speculations have greatly enriched the tale and made it the most elaborately examined political episode of the past century. Yet paradoxically, all these studies have also exacerbated debate about the motivations of the Soviet and American leaders who produced, managed, and finally resolved the crisis.

I dare to add my own retelling of the tale from a distance of forty years because I have found in the growing literature much fascinating detail to enlarge my contemporary experience of the crisis and to confirm my understanding of its major elements—why the crisis occurred, how it played out, and how close the world came to nuclear war.

I write with the memories of a reporter who covered the crisis as it unfolded, for *The New York Times* in Washington. I also write and reflect with the experience of covering the diplomacy and politics of John

F. Kennedy's Washington, Fidel Castro's Havana, and Nikita S. Khrushchev's Moscow, experiences that entailed close observation of most of the principals in this story. And I have freely exploited the extensive library produced by the crisis: dozens of histories and memoirs, works of intense scholarship, and the oral testimony evoked at multiple reunions of some of the Soviet, American, and Cuban antagonists. That the record remains incomplete and at times contradictory should be neither surprising nor discouraging; human history cannot escape the complexity of human thought and deed.

The books and documents to which I am most indebted are listed in the bibliography. But gratitude and fairness require a special, upfront tribute to James G. Blight, David A. Welsh, and Bruce J. Allyn, who labored to arrange the reunions of crisis participants, to record and annotate their exchanges, and to wean important, albeit incomplete documentation from Cuban and former Soviet archives. Equally essential to any review of the crisis are the recordings of White House meetings made by President Kennedy and transcribed under the leadership of Timothy Naftali, Philip Zelikow, and Ernest May (with important supplementary corrections by Sheldon M. Stern, the former historian at the John F. Kennedy Library). Yet even that massive record requires the balance of once secret documents brought to light through the persistent work of the National Security Archive in Washington and of Timothy Naftali and Aleksandr Fursenko in Moscow. My interpretations at times differ from theirs, but their masonry of fact has left an indispensable foundation for all who follow.

—M. F.

HIGH NOON IN THE COLD WAR

ONE

THE CRISIS IN MEMORY

For most Americans who experienced it, or relived it in books and films, the Cuban Missile Crisis is a tale of nuclear chicken—the Cold War world recklessly flirting with suicide.

We remember a bellicose Soviet dictator, who had vowed to bury us, pointing his missiles at the American heartland from a Cuba turned hostile and communist.

We remember a glamorous president, standing desperately against the threat, risking World War III to get the missiles withdrawn.

We remember the Russians blinking on the brink, compelled to retreat by a naked display of American power, brilliantly deployed, unerringly managed.

The crisis was real enough, but for the most part, we remember it wrong.

No episode of the last century has been so elaborately documented, so often reenacted in print and on film, and so many times earnestly reexamined at extraordinary reunions of Russian, American, and Cuban veterans of the drama.[1] As one of them, McGeorge Bundy, has observed, "forests have been felled to print the reflections and conclusions of participants, observers and scholars" of the crisis. And most recently, their views and recollections have been augmented by voluminous government records of the United States, some from old Soviet archives, and even a few from Cuban dossiers.

Yet over the decades, even the most attentive scholars and participants kept debating the main questions surrounding this sensational event. They failed to agree on why it happened, and they lacked the facts about how it really ended. And they have still not overcome the popular misconceptions about the motives and conduct of the two Cold War antagonists—Nikita Khrushchev, the wily old peasant ruling the Soviet empire, and John F. Kennedy, the jaunty young president leading the Western democracies. Nor have the many histories overcome the temptation to enrich the drama with alarmist claims that these two supercharged men came within hours, even minutes, of igniting an all-out nuclear war.

The fear of war during the crisis week of October 22–28, 1962, was palpable, in the Kremlin as in the White House. It was even greater among populations that could read uncensored accounts of the chilling, intimidating rhetoric with which Khrushchev and Kennedy bargained for concessions to resolve the crisis. Yet with all the information now available, it is clear that Khrushchev and Kennedy were effectively deterred by their fear of war and took great care to avoid even minor military clashes. In the end, both were ready to betray important allies, resist the counsel of chafing military commanders, and endure political humiliation to find a way out of the crisis. Their anxiety was real. But with the benefit of time and distance from the emotions of the Cold War, we can now see

---

[1] I use *Russian*, as did most Americans, as a euphonious, interchangeable shorthand for "Soviet" citizens, well aware that only half that union's people were actually Russian in nationality or ethnicity.

that their reciprocal alarm kept them well away from a nuclear showdown.

Time and distance also serve to illuminate the causes of the fateful events of 1962 that Americans call the Cuban Missile Crisis.[2]

As I first sensed in reporting from Moscow at the height of Khrushchev's power, his pugnacity was born of a typically Russian insecurity. His most aggressive actions against the West tended to mask a deeply defensive purpose. The evidence now available, though still debated, shows that it was to offset a debilitating weakness, not to imperil America, that Khrushchev careered into the crisis.

And as I slowly learned in covering Kennedy's Washington, the imperative of protecting himself politically inevitably shapes a president's perception of the nation's security. The cumulative record shows that Kennedy's decision to challenge the Soviet missiles in Cuba was rooted in a need to prove himself, more even than in any threat posed by the missiles themselves. Yet in reporting the day-to-day events of the crisis, and reading the many Washington-centered accounts in later years, I never fully appreciated the extent of Kennedy's statesmanlike restraint in steering his team to a diplomatic resolution. Though haunted by domestic critics, he nonetheless weighed every move with respect for his adversary and showed a decent regard for the opinions of other affected nations and the judgment of history.

Luck played a role in averting disaster, in preventing events from racing out of control. The crisis owed its origin to miscalculation, misinterpretation, and misjudgment. Yet the record now available shows that once they understood their predicament, two dissimilar statesmen commanding disparate societies reasoned their way back to a recognition that nothing vital, nothing truly affecting their nations'

---

[2] The Soviets called it the Caribbean Crisis, to imply that confrontations elsewhere were equally serious and that U.S. actions, not their missiles, were the source of the trouble. Cubans still call it the October Crisis, by way of complaining that they experience almost monthly crises in relations with the United States.

well-being was at stake. Unlike Fidel Castro, the charismatic and dogmatic Cuban leader around whom the crisis swirled, they had no desire to sacrifice lives to a Pyrrhic cause.

Now that we can peer into the minds of both the Soviet and American leaders at a crucial junction, the story of the Cuban Missile Crisis shifts from a merely fateful dance at the nuclear brink to a truly great drama. It is a tale of intricate, psychological combat, of men beating a path from dangerous ignorance to enlightened awareness, defining their values and preserving their balance in the midst of a storm. Driven by fear of the inhuman power they had to share, they found, if only for a moment, a shared humanity and yen to survive.

TWO

THE PALMS OF SPRING

I T ALL BEGAN WITH A RUSSIAN PLOY WORTHY OF THE HORSE at Troy, in the summer of 1962. In great haste, the rulers of a then mighty empire called the Soviet Union assembled a fleet of innocent-looking cargo ships, filled them with nuclear missiles, launchers, warheads, and other fearsome weapons, and sent them under false manifests across the seas to the newly communist island of Cuba. There, a secret army of forty thousand Soviet soldiers and technicians began furtively to erect the missiles at fortified bases, aiming them at the soft underbelly of the United States and expecting them to stand unnoticed among Cuba's majestic palm trees. Then, come November, the missiles were to be suddenly revealed by the Soviet and Cuban leaders as they embraced on the ramparts of Havana and shouted to shocked Americans, "Now let's negotiate—as equals!"

And they almost brought it off.

Only in mid-October, with the shipments not quite complete, did American spy planes and photo analysts detect a few of the construction sites and recognize nuclear rockets that could reach targets as far away as Washington, DC, Dallas, or the Panama Canal. These were precisely the kind of weapons that the Soviet leader, Nikita S. Khrushchev, had said he would never need to deploy outside his own country, hoping to lull his American adversaries until the missiles were armed and well defended. But his deceptions were precisely the kind of lies that the American leader, John F. Kennedy, felt he could not safely leave unpunished. And so the chairman of the USSR and the president of the USA stumbled into the scariest episode of the atomic age.

For seven portentous days in October 1962, they marched gravely toward one another, nukes drawn. It felt like High Noon in the Cold War.

ONCE HE ACQUIRED dictatorial power in the mid-1950s, Nikita Sergeyevich Khrushchev proved to be an adventurous leader trying to rush his people out of a Stalinist hell toward a brighter future. As he remembered years later, dictating his memoir, the idea of sending his missiles to Cuba just popped into his head one day in April 1962, while he strolled on the banks of the Black Sea with his minister of defense, Marshal Rodion Malinovsky, a comrade since the great World War II battle of Stalingrad. The bulldog-faced marshal was growling again about the American Jupiter missiles aimed at Soviet bases from neighboring Turkey, just across the water.

Well then, Khrushchev wondered, why couldn't they do the same to the Americans—from Cuba? After sitting so long, so smugly behind their ocean moats, Americans should finally share the anxiety of living in the thermonuclear shadows that hung over all Europeans.

That neat symmetry—we Russians will do in Cuba what you Americans are doing in Turkey—made the idea especially appealing. It seemed morally justified, physically reciprocal, and eminently legal. The Americans might object, but they had no good reason to feel injured or weakened.

Khrushchev's memoir notwithstanding, however, the missile deployment was no momentary whim. He had floated the idea weeks earlier to his closest colleague in the Soviet oligarchy, Anastas Mikoyan. And he had hinted at it in early March, while chatting with his new ambassador to Washington, Anatoly Dobrynin. After noting that the future of Germany was still the main issue in U.S.–Soviet relations, Khrushchev displayed his resentment of America's nuclear superiority—and of those damn bases in Turkey "under the very nose of the Soviet Union."

"It's high time their long arms were cut shorter," he told Dobrynin.

We now know, thanks to the recollections of his son, Sergei Khrushchev, himself once a Soviet missile engineer, that the chairman and Marshal Malinovsky faced a much greater problem that spring than a few American rockets in Turkey. They had learned, in a February council of war, that Soviet long-range nuclear weapons, the kind that could reach from Soviet territory all the way into the United States, were doomed to remain inferior to America's for many years. The "imperialists," as Khrushchev liked to call Americans, could outgun him ten times over.

Soviet rocket scientists had reported that their designs and tests of intercontinental ballistic missiles (ICBMs) had hit multiple snags. Two dozen prototypes were impossibly slow to rev up for firing and extremely hard to aim with accuracy. The only available fuels were so volatile that the missiles could not be kept ready for launch or counted on to elude an attack from the much more numerous American forces.

This bitter news meant that Khrushchev's colorful boasts, over many years, that he was churning out missiles "like sausages" and that they could hit "a fly" eight thousand miles away were just so much empty bluster. In fact, the bluffing had become self-defeating. It had inspired the Americans to produce better weapons so that they no longer had to fear his blustering diplomacy. Worst of all, the missile deficit threatened Khrushchev's desire to turn tanks and destroyers into plowshares—to shift rubles from the military budget to the production of desperately needed food and consumer goods.

The Soviet leader and his defense minister obviously needed a quick and inexpensive path around their predicament. American rockets and bombers could deliver so many nuclear warheads to Soviet targets that they could easily overwhelm Russia's small retaliatory force. Without effective long-range missiles, Khrushchev had to rely on vulnerable, long-distance bombers that lacked America's technology for midair refueling and could reach the United States only with suicidal missions.

Khrushchev did, however, possess hundreds of effective medium-range missiles. He had indeed turned them out like sausages, aimed them at British, French, and German cities, and invoked them often in support of his assertive European policies. Now that Cuba was available as a launching platform conveniently anchored off the Florida coast, these medium-range missiles could instantly serve an intercontinental function. For the modest cost of transporting some of the missiles to Fidel Castro's island, Khrushchev could double the reach of the Soviet nuclear forces.

A deployment to Cuba would not come close to matching America's firepower. Still, in these early years of the nuclear age, the threat of even a few rockets that could reliably strike American cities in minutes would achieve a crude balance of terror and serve to deter an attack on the Soviet Union. By providing a good defense for the missiles in Cuba and also basing some missile-firing submarines there, Khrushchev thought he would achieve a quick and cheap fix for an otherwise chronic weakness. In his apt metaphor, the deployment to Cuba would greatly lengthen Russia's nuclear arms.

ALWAYS RELUCTANT TO CONFESS a weakness, Khrushchev revealed his Cuban plan to only a few associates, and he shrewdly did it more in ideological than military terms. Instead of admitting a strategic necessity, he emphasized a desire to protect Fidel Castro's revolution against an obviously hostile United States. Kennedy had made no secret of his desire to overturn the Castro regime. After sponsoring a feeble attack by Cuban exiles a year earlier at Cuba's Bay of Pigs, the U.S. government was sure to mount another, more effective assault. A Soviet shield for Cuba would preserve a communist outpost in the Western Hemisphere and put an end to the Chinese taunts that the Soviet Union had turned into a "paper tiger."

Khrushchev so dominated the Soviet hierarchy in 1962 that even his wildest schemes quickly became policy. Only Anastas Mikoyan, his closest colleague in the Soviet Presidium, the nation's board of directors, expressed some doubts about the missile venture. Mikoyan had visited Fidel Castro two years earlier, admired his revolutionary zeal as reminiscent of his own radical youth, and favored him with Soviet trade and aid. But Mikoyan also deemed himself an expert on the United States. And he did not think a narrowly elected president and America's "ruling circles" would tolerate a Soviet nuclear fortress in their sphere of dominance. The Russians would be violating the hoary Monroe Doctrine, which Americans always invoked to justify the exclusion of European powers from their hemisphere.

Nonsense, Khrushchev retorted. That doctrine either worked both ways or not at all. America had certainly not kept out of Russia's neighborhood—just look at the bases in Turkey. Once the Soviet missiles were installed, the Americans would learn to live with them, he predicted; when he revealed the missiles in November, after their congressional elections, the Americans "will make a fuss, make more of a fuss, and then accept."

AN ENTIRELY DIFFERENT DOUBT about the scheme came from Aleksandr Alekseyev, a Spanish-speaking Soviet agent who had befriended Castro in Havana while masquerading as a journalist. When

Khrushchev asked his advice in late April, Alekseyev predicted that the Cubans would refuse to cooperate. They prized their independence and would fear losing face among Latin revolutionaries if they let their island become a Soviet missile platform.

Where others saw obstacles, Khrushchev saw challenge. He thought he knew how to prevent a Cuban veto. In early May, he crowned Alekseyev as his next ambassador to Havana and so informed Castro in a warm, expansive letter. Khrushchev promised, finally, to send Fidel the many defensive weapons he had requested months earlier. And he planned also to send additional weapons, best left undescribed in writing, which he held out as absolutely essential for Cuba's defense. The arms shipments would cost Cuba nothing. Moreover, all prior debts to the Soviet Union were now forgiven. Please therefore prepare to welcome Ambassador-designate Alekseyev and the "irrigation and land reclamation delegation" that was coming with him.

The real boss of this delegation turned out to be Marshal Sergei Biryuzov, the head of Soviet rocket forces, traveling in disguise as "Engineer Petrov." And contrary to all predictions, the marshal made an easy sale.

Castro did not agree with the argument that Cuba needed nuclear missiles to defend itself. He would have been satisfied with a treaty of alliance or a few Russian troops serving as a sort of trip wire to engage the Soviets in any war with America. Indeed, Castro felt strongly, as Alekseyev had predicted, that harboring Soviet missiles would compromise his reputation for independence and tarnish his image in Latin America. He nonetheless readily accepted Khrushchev's plan. He thought it would "buttress the defensive power" of the entire communist bloc. Fidel conferred briefly with his associates, and all were pleased to be of service to the world communist cause. Tarnished or not, they were delighted to play a prominent part in the East–West struggle. They could hardly wait to thumb their noses at the menacing *Yanquis* from behind Soviet nuclear rockets.

Maps in hand, Marshal Biryuzov and his "reclamation" team spent ten days surveying the island for the ports, sites, roads, and installations they would need to erect and defend the missile bases. When he returned to report that the missiles could be deployed in secret because they would be naturally camouflaged among clusters of Cuba's palm trees, Khrushchev, as Mikoyan scornfully recalled, "naturally, believed him." So did the rest of the Soviet leaders, who routinely smiled or frowned in concert with their leader. The most obviously eager were the Soviet military brass. When one general ventured to raise a doubt about the palm-tree disguise, Marshal Malinovsky silenced him with a swift kick to the shins.

NOW IT WAS TIME for the Russians to apply their logistic genius, the improvisation skills that served so often to overcome the cruelest climate and fiercest enemies. Despite the Soviet Union's military prowess, the nation that I covered as a reporter in Khrushchev's day barely deserved the reputation of superpower. It lacked elementary roads and communications, failed to grow enough food in soil that had once been the breadbasket of Europe, and left millions of people scrambling after a bar of soap or roll of toilet paper. Yet in June 1962, with startling speed, the regime assembled and equipped a fleet of eighty-five vessels that would make 150 trips to a distant shore, ferrying weapons and equipment for the construction of dozens of installations and the deployment of an entirely self-sufficient nuclear army—all the while disguising the fleet's true mission and the nature of its deadliest cargoes.

The first disguise was a code name. They called it Operation Anadyr, after a river and territory in remote northeastern Siberia, as far from subtropical Cuba as a Russian bear could crawl. Not even the captains of the first wave of merchant ships knew their destination until they opened sealed orders well out to sea. In preparing embarkations out of seven Soviet ports, the soldiers, stevedores, and deckhands labored in fenced compounds guarded by the KGB, the Soviet secret police. To mislead gossips and spies, many of the troops were issued fleece-lined parkas, felt boots, even some skis, before they learned in midvoyage that they would be wearing civilian trousers and sport shirts in a tropical heat.

Never before had Russians attempted a deployment of such mystery and complexity. The first ships set off in early July, misrepresenting their cargoes and destination on public manifests. When foreign pilots tried to come aboard to guide some of the ships through the Turkish Straits, they were waved off, offered not the customary ladders but gifts of vodka and caviar.

Some of the vessels had to be totally refitted to house missiles that had never been shipped outside Soviet territory. The accommodations for Cuba-bound troops and technicians were even less suitable. As one Soviet general recalled, the soldiers spent twenty days at sea packed like sardines in floating steel boxes under a broiling sun. Small groups of them could come up on deck only briefly at night "for a few minutes of exercise and a gulp of fresh sea air." Seasickness felled half the travelers. Many of their uniforms were ruined by mildew. A two-month supply of butter melted en route.

THE SOVIET BASES IN CUBA were designed to house two types of missile. In the first wave of shipments came twenty-four mobile launchers with thirty-six missiles—the R-12, which Americans designated an SS-4. It was a medium-range ballistic missile, or MRBM, capable of threatening the entire southern United States to a range of about eleven hundred miles.

Later shipments would bring sixteen fixed-site launchers with twenty-four missiles. This weapon, the R-14—called an SS-5 in the West—was an intermediate-range ballistic missile, or IRBM. Its range of twenty-two hundred miles posed a threat to all but the farthest northwest corner of the United States.

In all, the plan called for forty launchers with sixty nuclear missiles—more than doubling the number of American targets that Soviet missiles could hope to strike from their own territory. The warheads in Cuba were to have explosive yields ranging from two hundred to eight hundred kilotons, more than ten to forty times the power of the atomic bomb dropped on Hiroshima.

In addition, Khrushchev envisioned using Cuba as a base for seven Soviet submarines, each capable of lobbing three R-13 nuclear missiles to a range of 350 miles. For naval defense, he sent four attack submarines, each carrying one nuclear-tipped weapon among its dozen torpedoes.

Such Soviet weaponry had never been shipped into alien waters. If threatened with capture, the fleet captains were to dump their missile cargoes at sea. No Cubans were allowed anywhere near the landing docks or construction sites. And to keep the weapons out of American (and Cuban!) hands, they were to be surrounded by a potent combination of air, land, and sea forces.

To guard against air attack, the Soviets planned to ring the island with 144 antiaircraft launchers, each supplied with four non-nuclear rockets. This weapon, a SAM (surface-to-air) missile called an SA-2 in Washington, had recently proved effective in bringing down high-flying American spy planes from an altitude of seventy thousand feet.

To protect all the missile installations, the Soviet planners hastily requisitioned long lists of other weapons:

- 40 MiG-21 fighter jets, to enhance the force of 40 lesser MiGs previously given to Castro.
- 4 motorized regiments of 2,500 men each, equipped with 124 battle tanks, 240 armored personnel carriers, 36 anti-tank mis-

siles, and 6 Luna artillery launchers capable of firing either conventional or nuclear shells.

- Naval forces that included 2 cruisers and 4 destroyers, 12 PT boats firing 24 short-range missiles, and 16 coastal cruise launchers whose 80 missiles could deliver nuclear warheads to a range of 40 miles.
- 42 IL-28 light bombers, most carrying torpedoes and mines, a few fitted to drop nuclear bombs.

And to service this elaborate expeditionary force, Soviet depots poured forth boatloads of supporting matériel, including:

- 3 hospitals of 200 beds each and an anti-epidemic detachment.
- 7 warehouses with a 3-month supply of food and fuel, plus a field bakery.
- Ammunition stores, maintenance shops, repair shops, and mobile fuel tanks.
- 20 prefab barracks and 10 wooden houses.
- 120 dump trucks, 20 bulldozers, 10 mobile cranes, 10 graders, and 10 excavators.
- 2,000 tons of cement and 6 cement mixers.
- Hundreds of tents, miles of cable and fencing, and tools and screws for every task.

Clearly, the unsung heroes of Operation Anadyr were the dozens of harbormasters who loaded these shipments at breakneck speed and launched them to arrive in the order they would be needed.

A few of the forty thousand Soviet troops and technicians were able to enjoy the voyage disguised as tourists on passenger ships. But most had to endure heaving storms and stinking heat, out of sight of the curious American planes that hovered overhead. On arrival in Cuba, the entire force was entrusted to the command of General Issa Pliyev, a cavalry veteran who had most recently earned Khrushchev's gratitude by forcefully suppressing food riots in Novocherkassk. The general's lack of rocket experience seemed at first to provide an extra bit of camouflage for the missile deployment. But Pliyev also lacked subtlety and tact, and he hated having to function in Cuba as "Ivan Pavlov," a commonplace pseudonym assigned to him by some bureaucrat.

Maybe that is why at the peak of the crisis, when he was most urgently needed at his post, the prideful Pliyev could not be found, and so unwittingly hastened his country's humiliation.

THREE

THE MISSILES OF OCTOBER

A S THE SOVIET MISSILES WERE BORNE ACROSS THE Atlantic in July 1962, President Kennedy was devouring and preaching from Barbara Tuchman's new history, *The Guns of August*. It taught him how misinformation and miscalculation and "some damned foolish thing in the Balkans" in 1914 had produced the first of the twentieth century's worldwide bloodlettings. He was telling colleagues to study the book because he took it to be a president's highest duty in the nuclear age to prevent similar misjudgments. As Kennedy later put it, he did not want to become a central character in a future bestseller called *The Missiles of October*.

A worthy caution but a vain ambition.

For at that very moment, both Khrushchev and Kennedy were committing equally disastrous miscalculations. Kennedy had decided that the Soviets would never deploy nuclear weapons to Cuba; Khrushchev had decided that the Americans would surely acquiesce in their deployment. And so jointly, with the help of some foolish bases in Turkey (near those Balkans), they miscalculated themselves into a flaming crisis.

. . .

IN CUBA ITSELF, Fidel Castro, the flamboyant radical of the Western Hemisphere, played only an incidental role in the weeks leading to crisis. He resented the secrecy surrounding the missile deployment and hoped that his military alliance with Moscow could be quickly publicized to deter American interference. He sent his brother, Raúl, to Moscow in July to negotiate a treaty of "mutual defense." As finally written, it pledged both countries to "take all necessary measures to repel" aggression against Cuba. Although this fell far short of promising that an attack on Cuba would be treated as an attack on the Soviet Union, Castro deemed it an ample gift. He sent another intimate, Che Guevara, to Moscow in August to beg Khrushchev to advertise the missile pact. Why hide an alliance and a deployment that were legal, unthreatening, and the right of any sovereign nation?

Khrushchev, however, insisted on secrecy. He claimed a better understanding of Americans and wanted to treat them to a surprise in November. He felt sure that Kennedy, always hypersensitive about a hostile Cuba and especially so during an election season, would blockade or attack the island if he knew what was coming. But once confronted by functioning missiles after Election Day, he would calm down and acquiesce. Khrushchev planned to send the president a confidential notice of the missiles in November, then visit the United Nations and fly on to Cuba to pose beside his rockets with Fidel. Who would then dare attack?

Still, the Cubans wondered uneasily, what would happen if the missiles were discovered before they were fully installed? Castro remembered Che Guevara rolling his eyes skyward at what he took to be Khrushchev's feeble response—that he would then "send the Baltic fleet." This did not sound like much of a match for American power. But perhaps the Soviet leader was in earnest, thinking that the missile-firing subs and battleships that were to follow his rockets to Cuba could pierce an American blockade and deter an invasion.

Though they felt diminished by the secrecy, the Cuban leaders resisted temptation to leak news of the Soviet project. To clear the designated missile sites, they chased thousands of their citizens out of their homes and jobs on false pretenses. They made excuses for keeping Cubans out of the freshly fenced Russian compounds. They even "quarantined" Cuban officers who had seen too much and volunteered to be isolated to avoid suspicion that they might betray the true nature of the installations.

Still, the Castro brothers could barely contain their excitement and pride and kept dropping hints of their incipient power. Castro himself asserted at the end of July that "the last danger" to his revolution was about to disappear. In mid-September, his official newspaper headlined the news that "Rockets Will Blast the United States If It Invades." And Castro's pilot, warning that "they don't know what is awaiting them," blabbered a drunken boast about nuclear missiles, which agents duly reported to the CIA in late September.

Hundreds of other reports reaching Washington mentioned missiles, but they were discounted by disbelieving analysts because the sources were failing to discriminate between non-nuclear, "defensive" antiaircraft rockets and clearly "offensive," longer-range nuclear weapons. Only a few agents in Cuba sent word of strange seventy-foot-long tubes that had never been seen outside the Soviet Union; they were spotted rumbling after dark through small towns east of Havana on trucks so cumbersome that they knocked over lampposts when turning corners.

But these telltale signs of MRBMs floated to Washington in a stream of plainly inaccurate rumors and agitations among Cuban refugees. And because they were unexpected, the missiles went undetected—for two or three weeks longer than necessary. Indeed, in its eagerness to avoid a clash with the Russians, the Kennedy White House actually hampered its own reconnaissance operation over Cuba.

· · ·

THE SOVIET CAMPAIGN TO DECEIVE the United States was begun
by Khrushchev himself, playing yet again on America's vulnerability
in West Berlin, the noncommunist half of the former German capital.
At a farewell picnic for his favorite Western diplomat, Ambassador
Llewellyn "Tommy" Thompson of the United States, the Soviet
leader offered heartfelt hugs to Jane Thompson and their children
while dropping sly hints that the year would end with another international crisis. Thompson was led to believe the crisis would be about
Berlin.

For the generation that fought World War II, Berlin symbolized
the costly allied victory over the Nazis, the subsequent division of
Germany, and the Cold War division of all Europe into two military
camps. The rival Western and communist armies now stood toe to
toe across the heart of Germany and also across the middle of Berlin,
whose western half had become a democratic island a hundred miles
inside Soviet-run eastern Germany. West Berlin would have slowly
faded into its communist surroundings had Stalin not tried to strangle it with a blockade of ground traffic in 1948. Alarmed by other Soviet advances in Europe, the United States broke the blockade with an
extraordinary airlift of an average six hundred flights a day, seven days
a week, which kept the city supplied with food and fuel for nearly a
year. When East Germany's hunger for trade with the West finally
caused it to reopen the roads to truck traffic, West Berlin still stood
free, all the more revered by Americans as a trophy of forceful, nonviolent resistance to Soviet expansion.

With the creation of two German nations, anomalous Berlin acquired the additional burden of preserving the German dream of reunification, which was strongly endorsed by the United States. But
for the Soviet Union, West Berlin represented unfinished business;
the free half of the city was an annoying lure for East German
refugees and an emblem of America's refusal to ratify the permanent
division of Germany and all Europe. Khrushchev solved the refugee

problem by building a wall through the center of Berlin in 1961, but he kept threatening the West's access to the city so as to compel the signing of a peace treaty that would forever secure the frontiers of communist East Germany.

From 1958 on, every Soviet deadline for altering the status of West Berlin had evoked a stronger American commitment to resist. Yet the only meaningful defense of that isolated territory was an American threat to defend it at all costs, with nuclear weapons. And threatening nuclear war for such a small piece of terrain was never entirely credible. Kennedy, like Khrushchev, often wondered whether his European allies would support such risk-taking for a largely symbolic German outpost. As Ambassador Thompson reported, Khrushchev "always felt he had us over a barrel" in Berlin. To which the president replied, "Yeah—and he's always been right."

Therefore, whenever he thought of resisting Soviet moves into Cuba, Kennedy's thoughts turned immediately to his vulnerability in Berlin. That vulnerability was both military and diplomatic. If he used force in Cuba, he risked provoking Soviet retaliation in Berlin. And if he made concessions in Berlin and Germany to obtain more security for the United States, he risked undermining the trust of the European allies in America's commitment to their defense.

Kennedy actually confessed his sense of vulnerability in Berlin directly to the Soviet leader in the private letters they exchanged through 1962. When Khrushchev cutely asked the president to please stop harassing Cuba-bound merchant ships with low-flying reconnaissance planes, Kennedy not only agreed to call a halt but dared to beg a favor in return: that the Russians put Berlin "on ice." A puzzled Khrushchev had to summon linguists to translate that cool idiom. Once he understood, he sent the president a patronizing promise that he would do nothing to "complicate the international situation or aggravate tension" during the 1962 congressional election campaign. The Berlin–Cuba connection thus became explicit and even more strongly embedded in Kennedy's mind.

.   .   .

AND AS KHRUSHCHEV WELL KNEW, the American election campaign had generated a lot of heat about the heavy Soviet traffic to
Cuba. Desperate to add to their meager thirty-six seats in the Senate
and 40 percent minority in the House of Representatives, leading Republicans were making the "loss" of Cuba to Soviet arms and influence their No. 1 campaign issue. Even before they actually knew the
dimensions of the Soviet deployment, they clamored for a blockade,
or invasion, to prevent it.

The direst warnings of a nuclear threat in Cuba came from Senator Kenneth Keating of New York, who claimed to have certain
knowledge about the Soviet buildup but refused to reveal his sources
even to the CIA. He was probably being briefed by Cuban refugees in
Florida, who relayed reports and speculations from the island and
progressively convinced him that Soviet missiles and combat troops
had been unloaded there. In late summer, the senator whipped up
alarmist headlines by chastising the president for tolerating a missile
buildup.

Skepticism about Keating's claims, clear up to the White House,
was rooted in the belief that the Russians would never risk sending
nuclear weapons so far from home. And the doubts were reinforced
by the fact that the earliest sightings by agents inside Cuba—and also
by spy planes from above—were of SAMs, the non-nuclear antiaircraft rockets that Khrushchev shrewdly ordered to be the first
weapons deployed. Although the SAM units had orders not to fire at
American planes, Khrushchev hoped that they would scare off the
U-2s and deny them photographs of the nuclear missiles as they arrived.

The chairman's hope was realized better than he knew. At the
worst possible moment, in excessive fear of causing an "incident" with
the Russians, the Kennedy team severely curtailed its U-2 reconnaissance flights over Cuba. Just as the missiles were going up, Washington pulled its blindfold down.

·   ·   ·

IN THE EARLY NUCLEAR YEARS, the U-2 spy-in-the-sky had been
the most reliable guardian of American security, a dazzling techno-
logical response to the psychological strain evoked by the Soviet
Union's missile prowess. A single-seat, single-engine, gliderlike jet
with a seventy-foot wingspan, the U-2 could safely traverse Soviet
territory at a height of more than thirteen miles, comfortably beyond
the reach of conventional antiaircraft weapons or fighter planes. And
aboard this remarkable craft were equally remarkable cameras, which
brought back such clear films of missiles and other military targets
that analysts could count and measure them with great precision.

In President Eisenhower's second term, from 1957 through 1960,
two dozen U-2s flew unmolested across Soviet airspace and provided
indisputable evidence that the United States held an overwhelming
advantage over the Soviets in deliverable nuclear weapons. The U-2
intrusions infuriated the Russians, but they satisfied Eisenhower that
he could deter any Soviet aggression with his threat of "massive retaliation." And the U-2s confirmed that despite Khrushchev's conspicuous success in vaulting *sputnik* capsules and cosmonauts into orbit,
America's strategic superiority was continuing to grow.

But the U-2's invincibility reached a bitter end on May Day, 1960,
when a Soviet SA-2 missile exploded close enough to finally force one
out of the sky. Khrushchev, who cherished surprises, first revealed
only the bare news of the plane's demise, then sat back to enjoy the
lies out of Washington about a "weather plane" that "might have
strayed" a few miles over the Soviet border. I witnessed the joyous excitement in the Kremlin on May 7, when Khrushchev triumphantly
dropped the other shoe: news that farmers deep in the heart of Siberia
had not only found much of the U-2 wreckage but also captured the
parachuting pilot—alive!

Three days later, the foreign reporters in Moscow were summoned to Gorky Park to watch Khrushchev vent his anger at an un-
apologetic Eisenhower. I can still see the veins popping from the

chairman's neck as he stood atop a wobbly wicker chair, urging us to inspect the "criminal" evidence all around: a display of the U-2's films and maps, parts of its wings and engine, and the pilot's personal effects. Khrushchev called mocking attention to the poison-tipped pin with which he presumed the pilot, Francis Gary Powers, was supposed to kill himself after destructing his top-secret plane and equipment.

The U-2 affair shattered a still wary relationship between Khrushchev and Eisenhower. And when two pilots of a less intrusive, low-level reconnaissance plane fell into Russian hands a few weeks later, Khrushchev kept them prisoner until he could deliver them as a gift to the next president—who, as he hoped, was Kennedy, not Richard Nixon, a chronic hater of everything Soviet. Powers, the U-2 pilot, was tried for espionage but he, too, was finally released to Kennedy in 1962, in a trade for a high-ranking Soviet spy.

By then, fortunately, the job of photographing Soviet territory had passed to untouchable satellites, cruising in orbit and equipped with even more sophisticated cameras. But the U-2s still performed useful service, photographing countries like China that were not yet fully covered from orbit. The planes also flew near the Soviet northern and eastern frontiers to gather samples of fallout from nuclear tests. And weather permitting, U-2s flew the length of Cuba twice each month in the summer of 1962, filming military installations and contributing to the Pentagon's contingency planning for attacking the island. It was one of these routine flights, on August 29, that first detected the hasty construction of eight Soviet antiaircraft SAM sites in Cuba's western province, Pinar del Río.

The discovery aroused curiosity in Washington but no great alarm. The Russians had often shipped SAMs to client states, notably Syria, Indonesia, and Egypt, as well as to Communist China. At this point, the Kennedy administration cared less about the new sighting than about avoiding another embarrassing "U-2 affair" with the Russians. For in early September, a U-2 had drifted accidentally into Soviet airspace in the Pacific and another, piloted by a Taiwanese, had been shot down over Communist China. To protect its reconnaissance operations and to avoid provoking the Russians, the White House ordered the U-2s to avoid Cuban airspace and to take only oblique-angle photos of the island. American intelligence thus went blind for five crucial weeks.

EVEN WITHOUT U-2 EVIDENCE, however, one ranking American official thought he saw through the Soviet buildup in Cuba. In the last days of August, John McCone, the head of the Central Intelligence Agency, reasoned his way into Khrushchev's mind and decided that the huge ring of SAM antiaircraft batteries going up around Cuba could have only one purpose: to prevent the CIA's U-2s from spotting further deployments. And what, he asked himself, would Moscow want to hide? Tenaciously, McCone argued that the SAMs presaged the arrival of medium-range nuclear missiles, so as to significantly augment the Soviet ability to strike at American targets. The Russians were trying to close, or at least narrow, their missile gap.

McCone was the odd and, at sixty, old man out in the Kennedy administration. Though recommended by Robert Kennedy to head the CIA, he was a deeply conservative Republican much less willing than the president to engage the Soviet Union or to trust its assurances. An engineer with a shipbuilding fortune earned in World War II, he had begun government service at the Pentagon and risen to become head of the Atomic Energy Commission under Eisenhower. President Kennedy named him to the CIA after the Bay of Pigs fiasco in early 1961, gaining not only McCone's expertise but also the political cover afforded by his anti-Soviet views and closeness to Eisenhower.

McCone could therefore press his views of Soviet intentions with an obstinate sense of independence. He was sure he had Khrushchev figured out, notwithstanding the consensus—in his own intelligence agency—that the Russians were unlikely to break with precedent to

deploy nuclear weapons on foreign soil. Just before leaving for a honeymoon in late August, McCone personally warned the president of his
foreboding. And in cables from Paris and the French Riviera, he kept
imploring aides in Washington to demand more reconnaissance flights
over Cuba. In these "honeymoon cables," as they came to be known,
McCone refused to be impressed even by a formal National Intelligence Estimate, in mid-September, that explicitly rejected his surmise.

The backstage demands from such a persistent Republican, combined with the public attacks of Senate Republicans, became too great
a political challenge for Kennedy to ignore. Even if Khrushchev
posed no great threat in Cuba, the president felt driven to protect his
domestic flank. He needed first to assure the American public that he
had his eye on Castro. He needed also to promise the hawks in Congress that he would not let Cuba become an offensive military base.
And finally he needed to caution Moscow to restrain its buildup on
the island. Given these political imperatives, Kennedy devoted an entire day, September 4, to that triple task.

THE MICROPHONES HE HAD PLANTED in several White House locations record a president struggling that morning with his top foreign policy advisers to compose a short note to Khrushchev that
would explain away—without direct apology—the accidental intrusion of a U-2 "air sampler" in the Far East. The writing did not come
easy because the choice of words really involved a choice of policy:
whether to continue such flights, whether to reveal their purpose, and
whether candor was really owed the Soviet leader. Secretary of State
Dean Rusk was especially concerned about reinforcing Kennedy's
"credibility" with Khrushchev so that they could effectively communicate about other "tight things" such as Berlin and Cuba. The meeting was a foretaste of the tense letter-writing the group would need to
deal with the Cuban crisis in the ensuing weeks.

An hour later that September 4, the president sat down again with his brother Bobby, the attorney general, Defense Secretary Robert McNamara, Secretary of State Rusk, and National Security Adviser McGeorge Bundy to try to craft a public statement about the Soviet buildup in Cuba. The president wanted to parry the Republican criticism. Rusk, a tough but prudent statesman, wanted to reassure Latin Americans that Castro would not be allowed to menace them with his new Soviet weapons. And McNamara, a brilliant technocrat with always aggressive opinions, wanted to tell the Russians that even the older MiG fighter-bombers they had shipped to Cuba were worrisome; he thought they foreshadowed the arrival of ever more sophisticated weaponry.

Still, the group agreed with Bundy's view that, however annoying the buildup in Cuba, the Soviet shipments would be intolerable only if they brought surface-to-surface missiles that could fire nuclear warheads into the United States. Their arrival would mark a "turning point" in the Soviet deployment, from "defensive" to "offensive" weaponry.

Even now, however, the president dared to wonder: What if they did bring in surface-to-surface missiles? Bundy, an astute reader of the president's moods, caught his drift and expressed doubt that counteraction would be required even then. After all, America's deliverable nuclear weapons would continue to outnumber Russia's by at least fifteen to one. What would be the harm in having a few more hostile missiles stationed in Cuba?

But Rusk reminded Kennedy that the political and psychological pressure produced by "offensive" missiles in Cuba would be unbearable. The United States would simply have to act against them, although it might act prudently, in stages, using a "systematic blockade to weaken Cuba" before risking the "bloodbath" of invasion. Well, in that case, McNamara wondered, why not start challenging the buildup right away? Because, the president injected firmly, a blockade of Cuba was bound to provoke a Soviet blockade of Berlin. The president felt so naked in Berlin that he wanted to keep action against Cuba in reserve to use as retaliation for a Soviet challenge in Germany.

In the president's mind, as in Khrushchev's, the superpowers shared vulnerabilities. They were hostage to each other in Cuba and Berlin and were both maneuvering for moral high ground, to see which could appear the victim of the other's provocation.

So the White House conferees on that fateful September day strained to find language that would simultaneously (1) deny any great danger in the Soviet shipments to Cuba so far; (2) define which weapons they would indeed consider intolerably menacing; and (3) warn the Russians to avoid such unacceptable deployments. The president wanted the statement to demonstrate his alertness. He also wanted to share the available U-2 intelligence with congressional leaders because that would force Republican "gasbags" to spread more accurate information in their campaign speeches.

Rusk described all the Soviet weapons seen in Cuba as still "defensive." He also found no evidence of the claims that Cubans were working to subvert other Latin regimes. But Robert Kennedy endorsed McCone's intuition that Cuba would, sooner or later, become a strategic base for Soviet missiles and submarines, and that this would require an American blockade and invasion. Moscow had to be warned that the Monroe Doctrine remained alive, in spirit if not in law: Europeans, keep out! It was left to the less excitable Kennedy, the president, to observe that the Monroe Doctrine was nothing more than a rhetorical gimmick and that the Russians were not really "invading" the hemisphere—they had been legally invited, by a sovereign Castro regime.

A fly on the White House wall that day would have been amazed by the confusion of thoughts and voices at the president's table as the group edited a proposed public statement:

" 'Dangerously close to a violation of the Monroe Doctrine' [is a phrase that] would become the subject of endless conversation about what does constitute a violation and what does not. . . ."

"Well, the 'however' clause which immediately follows . . ."

"But what is the 'violation'? . . ."

"Others would say it's already been violated . . ."

"It's just whether the Soviet Union establishing bases here or putting missiles here, whether that is in fact an 'aggression' . . ."

"It depends a lot . . ."

"Well, we don't have to settle that question today . . ."

"At the bottom of page 4, 'limited to weapons normally associated with defense' . . . rather than say 'it will continue to be so confined' that 'it must be so confined'? . . ."

"Does that not mean you're going to confine it? . . ."

"Well, 'it will continue to be so confined' means, in this context, not negotiable . . ."

" 'Should it be otherwise, the greatest questions would arise for our friends in Latin America' . . ."

"Well, you want to be careful of making a threat to do something if they get some particular weapon . . ."

"Well, I would say ground-to-ground missiles . . ."

"But just saying 'offensive weapons' . . ."

"I don't know what an 'offensive weapon' is . . . That's a substantive question. . . ."

"You can't keep them out of international waters with their patrol boats so we're going to have to say 'any part of the hemisphere . . .' "

"The fact of the matter is," the president persisted, "the major danger is the Soviet Union with missiles and nuclear warheads, not Cuba. . . . This is not an aggressive danger to us except indirectly . . . as it now stands."

His attention exhausted by the hairsplitting, Kennedy anointed a drafting committee led by his deft speechwriter, Ted Sorensen, to winnow the mass of suggestions into something short and clear.

Meanwhile brother Bobby, as everyone called him, rushed to keep a date with the affable new Soviet ambassador, Anatoly Dobrynin, but he returned unenlightened, not yet realizing that Dobrynin knew even less than the White House about the Soviet project in Cuba.

WHEN THE PRESIDENTIAL TEAM reconvened, it was joined by CIA analysts, Latin and Soviet specialists, General Maxwell Taylor, the dapper new chairman of the Joint Chiefs of Staff, and General Curtis LeMay, the truculent air force commander. The group was beginning to congeal into a council of war for Cuba, but enlargement did not enhance its literary skills. Moreover, Kennedy kept wanting to explore the issues behind the rhetoric. He was especially eager to learn whether the arrival of Soviet SAMs now endangered more U-2 missions over Cuba. He also wanted to know whether the air force could really knock out the SAMs, if required, without incurring casualties. The president formed yet another drafting committee and went off to confront congressional leaders.

This meeting, too, became a tense semantic struggle, mainly over the president's distinction between "defensive" and "offensive" weapons. Senator Richard Russell of Georgia, the powerful Democrat and chairman of the armed services committee, observed sardonically that even a shotgun would be "offensive" if used to chase the navy out of its treasured base in Guantánamo Bay, on Cuba's southeastern coast. (Castro deeply resented that anomalous installation—an American leasehold "in perpetuity"—but he had not dared to challenge it militarily.)

As the Republican legislators demanded action, the president took refuge in his global view. He pleaded that "we are not talking about nuclear weapons" in Cuba, and please remember "we've got a very difficult situation in Berlin" and elsewhere. A blockade of Cuba, he warned, "is a major military operation, too; it's an act of war." Besides, a blockade would have to last many months to weaken Cuba and

"Berlin obviously would be blockaded also." The Berlin–Cuba equation in his mind had become obsessively firm.

The president dared also to portray the situation from Khrushchev's perspective. He told the legislators that "after all, the United States put missiles in Turkey—which are ground-to-ground, with nuclear warheads." He concluded by repeating that "the biggest danger right now is for Berlin." But he vowed, fatefully, that if ground-to-ground missiles did appear in Cuba, "the situation would then be quite changed and we would have to act."

Kennedy fully expected that he would never have to act on this pledge. It was intended only to cool off the campaign clamor. Moreover, a gentle public warning to Moscow would gain him credit for blocking a Soviet move that he did not in his deepest fears expect.

A statement to becalm the Republicans and to caution the Russians—in just one portentous phrase—had now been polished by Bundy and Sorensen. It was read out that September evening by Pierre Salinger, the White House press secretary: "There is no evidence of any organized combat force in Cuba from any Soviet bloc country, of military bases provided to Russia, of a violation of the 1934 treaty relating to Guantánamo, of the presence of offensive ground-to-ground missiles or of other significant offensive capability, either in Cuban hands or under Soviet direction and guidance. *Were it to be otherwise, the gravest issues would arise.*"

Conditions in Cuba, of course, were fast becoming otherwise.

KHRUSHCHEV GOT THE MESSAGE and read the president so well that he stepped on Kennedy's Berlin toe some more. From his vacation villa on the Black Sea, he summoned Stuart Udall, the American secretary of the interior then touring Russia, and let fly a litany of complaint and threat. Why did the president lack the courage to accept the Soviet position on Berlin? What was Berlin to the United States? And why was the Soviet Union surrounded by American military bases?

"Let's not talk about using force; we're equally strong," Khrushchev said. In fact, "we can swat your ass."

But the chairman had begun to worry that his missiles might be detected before they were fully installed and securely defended. He ordered Malinovsky to reinforce the ground troops assigned to Cuba. He even approved giving them a dozen nuclear artillery shells to resist or deter an invasion. Whether he would ever authorize their use was left unclear.

Khrushchev also amplified his deceptions, to test what Kennedy knew and to explore the word game the president had created. Maybe he could mollify the Americans by arguing that everything being sent to Cuba was, after all, "defensive." Khrushchev instructed Dobrynin and other emissaries to spread the word in Washington that Soviet shipments to Cuba had only a "defensive purpose." And he asked them to repeat the promise that nothing untoward was planned during the American election campaign.

These secret assurances, however, still left Kennedy vulnerable to Republican charges that he was neglecting the Soviet buildup. So the president flexed some muscle. He asked Congress for "stand-by authority" to call up 150,000 reservists and announced plans to stage amphibious maneuvers in the Caribbean, near Cuba, in mid-October. (In some Pentagon general's dyslexic jest, these maneuvers were proclaimed to be rehearsing the overthrow of a communist island's dictator, provocatively named "ORTSAC.")

And the more Khrushchev denied what he was doing, the more assertive Kennedy grew in vowing to resist what he was sure would never happen. *Guns of August* redux.

On September 11, Khrushchev formally replied to Kennedy's warning of "grave" consequences and embedded the message inside a four-thousand-word statement. It was a masterpiece of denial by evasion: "There is no need for the Soviet Union to shift its weapons for the repulsion of aggression, for a retaliatory blow, to any other country, for instance Cuba. Our nuclear weapons are so powerful in their explosive force and the Soviet Union has such powerful rockets to carry these nuclear warheads that there is no need to search for sites for them beyond the boundaries of the Soviet Union."

No need, of course, did not mean "no reason" or "no desire." In any case, Khrushchev's pained, lawyerly pretense of denial was almost lost in a rambling propaganda blast. Whereas Kennedy spent hours honing his diplomatic notes, the Soviet messages of that period were filled with Khrushchev's off-the-cuff locutions, lectures, assaults, and distortions, ranging from angry threats to oily claims of innocence. Even a summary of his "government statement" of September 11 can only hint at the full flavor:

To command the world's attention, it began with nothing less than a warning that American provocations "might plunge the world into the disaster of a universal world war with the use of thermonuclear weapons." By implication, it denied that Cuba had become a Soviet base yet it also explicitly justified such a base. It denounced Americans for complaining about "necessary commodities and food" going to "little heroic Cuba," but argued also that the content of Soviet shipments to Cuba was none of America's business—"Don't butt your noses where you oughtn't." Finally, in a condescending distraction, Moscow sympathized with the difficulty Americans always had waging diplomacy during an election campaign. But these elections were occurring all too often, it complained, and the time was near when ending the occupation of West Berlin and ratifying the division of Germany "must be accomplished—and it will be accomplished."

Despite the offensive Soviet tone, Kennedy accepted at face value the buried claim that Moscow had "no need" of nuclear weapons in Cuba and the claim, yet again, that Berlin was the real thorn in Khrushchev's hide. So the president felt emboldened at a September 13 news conference to turn up the heat on his Republican critics. He deplored their "loose talk" about attacking Cuba, arguing that it gave "a thin color of legitimacy to the Communist pretense that such a threat exists." Of course he would do "whatever must be done" if

Cuba ever became "an offensive military base of significant capacity for the Soviet Union." But moments later, he complained in a meeting with Orvil Dryfoos, the publisher of *The New York Times*, that people were "exaggerating" Cuba. The crunch, he was sure, was coming in December—but in Berlin.

The president was further misled by another private letter from Khrushchev explaining that he had raised the Berlin issue—after promising to let it lie "on ice"—only because the president had raised his voice about Cuba. "I must tell you straightforwardly, Mr. President, that your statement with threats against Cuba is just an inconceivable step. Under present circumstances, when there exist thermonuclear weapons, your request to Congress for authority to call up 150,000 reservists is not only a step making the atmosphere red-hot, it is already a dangerous sign that you want to pour oil on the flame."

THE FIRST OF THE SOVIET nuclear missiles reached the port of Mariel on September 15 aboard the *Poltava*, a ship observed by American reconnaissance to be riding suspiciously high in the water, as if carrying a large but relatively light cargo, namely missiles. A formal estimate by Washington's best analysts on September 19 took note of this anomaly and actually recited the strategic advantages to Moscow of placing medium-range missiles in Cuba. But the analysts went on to conclude that such a deployment would be "incompatible with Soviet practice to date and with Soviet policy as we presently estimate it."[3]

Not even overt lies could have done so well to mislead and confuse as the signals that Khrushchev and Kennedy sent flying across the At-

---

[3] Wryly mocking his own misjudgment years later, Raymond Garthoff, the State Department's expert on Soviet weaponry, observed that the American analysts had been right and Khrushchev's policy wrong; Washington had understood the *true* Soviet interest better than he.

lantic in late September. But Khrushchev worried that his missile ploy might be detectable and scratched two obviously "offensive" elements from the Cuba mission—the missile-firing destroyers and submarines. Kennedy, in turn, hedged against miscalculation by ordering the Pentagon to sharpen its contingency plans for attacking Cuba, even as he lobbied Congress to tone down a resolution it was writing to authorize the use of force against Castro.

The White House was not particularly disturbed to learn that crates containing IL-28 light bombers had now reached Cuba. But it did not appreciate the finger-wagging letters from Khrushchev. Why did he keep invoking the specter of nuclear war? His verbal missiles were sufficiently troubling for the president to seek instruction in a ninety-minute seminar from his most experienced Kremlinologists, Charles "Chip" Bohlen and Tommy Thompson, who had served as ambassadors in Moscow during the decade of Khrushchev's rise to power. They thought Khrushchev might be reacting to signs of Western weariness over Berlin; the French were openly saying the city was "withering on the vine." But they were sure that Khrushchev wanted above all to avoid war against the United States. He might even hope to provoke some belligerent American behavior so as to cool off hardliners in his regime. (This observation must have tickled Kennedy's sense of irony; he was spending much of that same day negotiating with the governor of Mississippi, who wanted to provoke the president into an intervention with federal troops to "compel" his state government to enroll James Meredith as the first black student in Ole Miss.)

Thompson predicted that even if Khrushchev finally signed the oft-threatened peace treaty with East Germany, he would still respect Western rights in Berlin rather than risk a military conflict. Thompson, too, considered Cuba a peripheral issue. He said it might help Khrushchev to understand Cuba's overheated place in American politics if he were reminded of the Kremlin's panic when Hungary briefly slipped from Soviet domination in 1956. Kennedy had invoked precisely that comparison in a conversation with Khrushchev's son-in-law but had succeeded only in arousing fears that he intended to oust Castro, just as Khrushchev had crushed the Hungarian rebels.

Khrushchev in any case well understood America's possessiveness about the Western Hemisphere. "Soon hell will break loose," he remarked at the end of September to Oleg Troyanovsky, an aide who grew up in Washington as the son of the first Soviet ambassador and who well understood American idioms and sensibilities.

"I hope the boat does not capsize, Nikita Sergeyevich," Troyanovsky cautioned.

Khrushchev merely ducked. "Now it's too late to change anything," he said.

DESPITE THE INCREASE in Soviet traffic into the Caribbean and Kennedy's response with maneuvers nearby, the president really did not intend to invade the island. He had organized an economic boycott of Cuba, sponsored sabotage against its enterprises, and encouraged attempts to assassinate Castro—all in the hope of somehow provoking an uprising. The Kennedy brothers insisted in private as well as public that Castro's removal was their highest priority. But they had drawn the line against an invasion to achieve it. They had no taste for a war that would have left them chasing Cuban guerrillas through the mountains for many bloody years. As Bundy put it, subversion was a politically useful substitute for invasion, not a preparation for it. All the contingency planning for an attack against Cuba was intended mainly to prepare a retaliatory blow in case the Russians squeezed too hard in Berlin.

Still, as McNamara confessed decades later, if he had been a Cuban looking north in those October days, "I think I might have expected a U.S. invasion." The United States had assembled formidable air, land, and sea forces in the South Atlantic. Congress passed its resolution authorizing force in support of "freedom-loving Cubans." The president was assured that he could safely knock out the Soviet SAMs because they could not cope with planes attacking at low altitudes. And McCone, back from his honeymoon, finally won his campaign for aggressive U-2 reconnaissance over all of Cuba.

WASHINGTON HAD PAID NO ATTENTION to a revealing clue dropped at the United Nations on October 8 by Cuba's president, Osvaldo Dorticós. He said Cuba was getting "inevitable weapons"—and surely his translator meant to say "ultimate weapons"—"the weapons which we would have preferred not to acquire and which we do not wish to employ." McCone, however, was now armed with reports of freshly arrived Soviet equipment in a quadrant of western Cuba that had not been overflown since late August. Russians were working furiously in newly turned soil there, and no Cubans were allowed anywhere near them. Wasn't it time to unleash the U-2s?

The White House finally lifted the restraints on U-2 missions on October 9. But cloudy weather and a shift of command from McCone's CIA to General LeMay's air force—resolving a long bureaucratic struggle—caused a further delay of five days. At last, on Sunday, October 14, while Kennedy was in Indianapolis mocking Senator Homer Capehart and other "self-appointed generals and admirals" for wanting "to send somebody else's son to war," Major Richard Heyser's U-2 flew for twelve minutes across western Cuba on a "milk run" devoid of incident and brought back four thousand feet of film that for Washington turned mystery into menace.

AT TEN O'CLOCK MONDAY, October 15, eight cans of film were delivered under armed guard to a shabby Washington office building whose top four floors belonged to the National Photographic Inter-

pretation Center. As vividly recounted by Dino A. Brugioni,[4] one of
its senior officials, the center soon produced unmistakable evidence of
medium-range missiles and launchers at two construction sites, and
probably at a third. The analysts employed primitive computers that
measured the missiles, apparently without warheads, to be sixty-seven
feet long. And that turned out to be the exact length of the R-12 missiles we foreigners had been allowed to photograph at May Day pa-
rades in Moscow. A similar but shorter-range missile was known to be
only fifty-four feet long. It was this thirteen-foot difference, as
recorded from a height of seventy-two thousand feet, that confirmed
the emergence of a significant threat to targets throughout the
United States.

The magnified, stereoscopic readings of the film were promptly
ratified by Arthur Lundahl, the center's inspired creator whose recruits had invented its many intelligence techniques. He passed the
news up the chain of command so that on Monday evening, senior officials could telephone furtively around Washington dinner parties to
say that "those things we've been worrying about" had indeed appeared in Cuba. Almost all who received these calls first uttered a disbelieving "Are you sure?"

Lundahl's team was very sure. But the CIA was at a loss to explain
why missiles so well concealed in transit and in Soviet rhetoric were
then left exposed under tarpaulins, without camouflage nets or other
concealing devices. Perhaps the answer was that there simply was no
hiding all the ancillary equipment. Tractors and trailers, fuel tanks,
trucks, cables, and concrete launching slabs were strewn about the
freshly churned terrain. The stupid prediction that palm trees could
hide the missiles had been compounded in Moscow by the failure to
reckon with the unavoidable surrounding clutter.

When given the disturbing news, McGeorge Bundy, the national

---

[4] Brugioni, Dino A. *Eyeball to Eyeball: The Inside Story of the Cuban Missile Crisis.*
New York: Random House, 1991.

security adviser, decided that a good night's sleep was the president's best preparation for crisis. He waited until Tuesday morning, October 16, to gather the revealing photographs and their interpreters at the White House. Even with a magnifying glass, Robert Kennedy could make no sense of the pictures; the telltale areas looked to him like scarred football fields. But he knew what the photos meant: "Oh shit! shit! shit! Those sons of bitches Russians." Fusing all of that week's troubles, he wondered bitterly whether the missiles could be aimed against the University of Mississippi.

At almost the same moment, Khrushchev in Moscow received a first visit from Foy Kohler, the new American ambassador, and repeated his bland assurances that the weapons going into Cuba were strictly "defensive." He regretted that Castro's loose talk about construction of a "fishing port" on the island had caused the president political difficulty and fear of a submarine base. The chairman did veer toward truth by remarking that he was not doing anything the Americans had not done to him—in Turkey and elsewhere. But there was time to talk things over after the election. He hoped to visit the United Nations in New York in November.

The election was not far from Kennedy's thoughts, either, as he sat at breakfast studying the troublesome U-2 photos. Beside him lay that morning's *New York Times*, whose lead story, from Kennedy's own Boston, was headlined, EISENHOWER CALLS PRESIDENT WEAK ON FOREIGN POLICY.

Once satisfied with the evidence of missiles, Kennedy listed the officials he wanted summoned to a council of war, cautioning all to observe the strictest secrecy until he decided how to deal with the situation. The men around him sensed a deep but controlled anger. The president obviously felt personally tested by Khrushchev's deceptions. Worse, the two leaders had misread each other. They had miscalculated themselves into an ugly confrontation. *The Guns of August* had spawned a sequel. Kennedy would after all be the hero, or villain, of *The Missiles of October.*

Outwardly, the president kept his cool and also his sense of irony. After a half-hour tour of the White House grounds with the family of astronaut Walter Shirra, he delivered the missile news to a disbelieving Kenneth O'Donnell, his special assistant, with acute political spin:

"You better believe it. We've just elected Capehart in Indiana—and Ken Keating will probably be the next president of the United States."

FOUR

K v. K

FOR THE ROOTS OF CRISES, LOOK TO POWERFUL MEN FEELING vulnerable and underestimated. Their dread of weakness, even imagined frailty, begets belligerence. Kennedy and Khrushchev led a cast of military millions and commanded horrific thermonuclear power in October 1962, yet they had to compete as lonely gladiators pulsing with fear—a fear of blundering into war, to be sure, but fear above all of being judged weak and wanting, in their own camp no less than in the adversary's. The Missile Crisis was also a Macho Crisis.

It was not, of course, a contest of equals. Kennedy, eloquent and handsome at forty-five, was a scion of wealth presiding regally over the democratic West. Khrushchev, a crude, peasant-born sixty-six-year-old, ruled imperiously over the communist East. Both had experienced World War II: Kennedy as the glamorous survivor of a sunken PT boat in the Pacific, Khrushchev as a Communist party commissar turning the tide against Hitler at bloody Stalingrad. The postwar Kennedy had waged an opportunistic campaign to make himself president, succeeding the highly popular General "Ike"

Eisenhower by narrowly defeating Ike's vice president, Richard Nixon. Khrushchev in that same time frame survived Stalin's brutality only by obeying the tyrant's evil whims and had to outfox his fellow henchmen to accumulate dictatorial power. Having mastered the old politics, both men pursued fitful reforms. Yet they found little comfort in success.

Covering Khrushchev for *The New York Times* at the height of his authority, from 1957 to 1960, I came to share Ambassador Thompson's view of him as much more complex and decidedly less menacing than the man we had all pictured from afar. He was ambiguity incarnate. He denounced Stalin—but selectively, mainly for crimes against fellow communists. He freed most political prisoners, but not quite all. He wanted to engage the outside world, but with strict limits and state controls. He slashed the size of the Soviet military, but refused to yield Soviet control over Eastern Europe.

Like most Americans, I first considered Khrushchev to be a colorful bully, a wily adversary determined to enlarge the Soviet empire. His tanks had brutally crushed a democratic uprising in Hungary in 1956. Still ringing in American ears was his menacing forecast of the West's destruction: "Whether you like it or not, history is on our side. We will bury you." As I eventually learned, all he meant was that Soviet communists would develop a superior social system and bear witness to the demise of capitalism. But decades passed before we learned that his diplomats and agents in Washington had his strict orders "to resist temptation when provoked."

"Don't ask for trouble," Khrushchev said to Ambassador Anatoly Dobrynin when he assigned him to the United States. "He plainly told me," Dobrynin remembered, "that I should always bear in mind that war with the United States was inadmissible—this was above all."

The product of ruthless, even demented politics under Stalin, Khrushchev somehow transformed himself into a reformer, one who harbored a romantic faith that communism could peacefully demonstrate its superiority over other forms of government. He really meant to pursue "peaceful coexistence" with the capitalist West and went out of his way to disown Stalin's dictum that war was "inevitable." Khrushchev often told his son, Sergei, that "communism was the best life for everyone, so why should we carry it to other countries on bayonets? Sooner or later they will understand and voluntarily follow us." His father's memories of war, the son recalled, "made the idea of starting yet another war, even with the 'best intentions,' unimaginable to him."

But it was hard for Americans to detect such sincerity in Khrushchev's periodic threats to hurl nuclear rockets at Western capitals, in his campaign to push the Western powers out of Berlin, and in his fitful support of anticolonial revolutions. Hardly any of his contemporaries recognized the defensive essence of his aggressive maneuvers. He ruled with a deep sense of inferiority, aware of the frailty of the Soviet "union" of nationalities. He feared a resurgent Germany. And he never outgrew his view of capitalists as predatory, like the British mine owners for whom he had labored in his youth.

Moreover, Khrushchev masked weakness with swagger and pursued his populist ambitions with authoritarian habits. But he also looked at the world with an insatiable, albeit undisciplined curiosity. He traveled widely beyond the Soviet frontiers and routinely exposed himself to Western reporters and diplomats in Moscow, boasting, joking, and wagging a chubby finger. Though squat, flabby, and bald, Khrushchev could affect a benign posture, except that his eyes rarely relented. And even his warmest smile was betrayed by two menacing moles on his cheek and steel caps on his back teeth. Khrushchev was no democrat but he was a fervent patriot who yearned to improve his people's living conditions. He dared to predict that the Soviet Union would overtake the United States in the production of meat, milk, and butter. Though a foolish forecast, it boosted morale by putting the Soviet economy in America's league. And it made credible his desire for peaceful, beneficial competition.

Like many smart peasants, Khrushchev was fascinated by technology. He had an optimist's certainty that there was a remedy for every problem and a despot's confidence that he could master any subject. The combination produced a restless impetuosity, a tolerance for risk, a disdain for dissent, and volatile surges of policy. He denounced Stalinist methods one month, reclaimed some the next. He invited free debate one day, suppressed it the day after. He seemed to know that stifling controls hog-tied a modern economy, but he could not shake the urge to wield central power. He designed convulsive economic reforms and reduced the privileges of bureaucrats and party satraps. But their regime survived him for another, fatally stagnant quarter century.

KHRUSHCHEV ROSE TO THE PEAK of his power during the Eisenhower years, while their governments struggled to adapt to the nuclear age. Each possessed overwhelming destructive power and therefore acquired acute new vulnerabilities. And although the Soviet Union and United States had few claims on each other, they were ideological antagonists and national rivals waging a "cold war" for influence around the globe. When Stalin imposed communist regimes on the nations of Eastern Europe to create a buffer zone against Germany, the West concluded that, like Hitler, he lusted to dominate the world and had to be contained if not driven back. When Chinese communists then seized power and joined North Korea's war against the United States, the menace of "international communism" appeared confirmed. That this "cold war" never turned fully hot was due primarily to the restraints imposed by the fear of nuclear devastation.

Both Soviet and American leaders believed at first that the mere threat of nuclear retaliation sufficed to deter attack; their populations were hostage to a balance of terror. But they soon learned that the number, style, and accuracy of nuclear weapons could confer a significant advantage, and this compounded their fears of an overpowering first strike by the adversary. A new stage in the arms race opened when Khrushchev momentarily won the race into space by successfully launching *sputnik* satellites into orbit in 1957. While American rockets were exploding in failure, he began to brag that his powerful rockets could reach the other side of the globe with deadly accuracy.

The motive for all this offensive swagger, however, was desperately defensive. The arms race was actually a crushing burden to him. The failures of Soviet agriculture and civilian industry had become self-perpetuating. Communist rule over the Soviet satellite regimes in East Europe had become expensive yet fragile. Hungary had almost escaped; Poland, Czechoslovakia, and Rumania palpably craved independence. And East Germany, which should have been the most advanced economy in the bloc, was bleeding refugees to prosperous, democratic West Germany. The Soviet effort to redraw the postwar map of Europe and to make a buffer of half the continent had turned into a costly, failing enterprise.

Starting in 1958, Khrushchev delivered repeated ultimatums to try to force the West to sign a "peace treaty" that would formally end World War II. He wanted it to divide Germany and fix its new frontiers forever, ceding territory to Poland in compensation for the Soviet seizure of Polish lands farther east. He wanted to crush the German dream of reunification, to make sure that Germany would never regain the strength to threaten Russia. And he wanted to stanch the flow of refugees out of communist East Germany to the West.

If the West refused to sign, Khrushchev vowed to block its access to Berlin—threats that merely confirmed America's view of him as an aggressor looking to undermine NATO and to dominate all Europe. He succeeded only in stiffening U.S. resistance and came away empty-handed from a visit to Eisenhower in 1959. Fearing further failure, Khrushchev scuttled a meeting with Western leaders in Paris in 1960 and decided to bet instead on the cooperation—or intimidation—of the next president.

. . .

KENNEDY, TOO, SAT WOBBLING on his throne. Besides the Soviet challenge in Germany and Berlin, he inherited a sluggish economy, a potential "missile gap" if the Russians chose all-out production of their huge rockets, a threat of communist advance in Southeast Asia, and the rapid communization of nearby Cuba. Moreover, he governed with a fragile mandate, having won the presidency by the narrowest of margins—less than one (sometimes dubious) vote per precinct—and only by faking youthful vigor and good health. At forty-three, he was the youngest man ever elected to the White House, but he was tormented most days by a crippling back injury, by colitis, and by the diminished function of the adrenal glands, called Addison's disease. He consumed a diet of multiple, competing drugs and was manipulated by multiple, competing physicians. Needing a daily dose of painkillers and often the secret help of crutches, he was hounded by thoughts of death and a shortened life.

Still, John Kennedy faced the world with extraordinary self-discipline and an ironic, self-deprecating humor, in notable contrast to Khrushchev's moody oscillations and belligerent wit. Kennedy had pursued the presidency during eight years as an undistinguished senator, driven to fulfill the ambition of a benighted, domineering father. But he had learned from a young age to think—and sin—for himself, to reject the old man's isolationism and his mother's pious Catholicism. Like Franklin Roosevelt, he was born to wealth but subscribed to the New Deal programs of mainstream Democrats. And he embraced the worldview of a bipartisan American "establishment," which was determined to prevent the expansion of communist power by shoring up anticommunist alliances in Europe and Asia.

Like most of his generation, Kennedy believed that the democracies' failure to resist Hitler's early aggressions in the 1930s had meant having to stop him in a catastrophic world war in the 1940s. And his generation applied this lesson by resolving to resist every expansionist impulse of the Soviet Union. Campaigning for president, Kennedy favored a strong national defense, but he criticized Eisenhower for relying too much on the retaliatory power of nuclear weapons. Since nuclear war had become unthinkable, Kennedy wanted more special forces that could resist communist advances in the early stages of conflict, especially unorthodox guerrilla challenges in poor regions.

On the eve of his inauguration, in January 1961, this outlook found reinforcement in a Khrushchev speech, which Kennedy read—and to some degree misread—through his preconceptions. The Soviet leader had addressed a conclave of communists from around the world with a passionate defense of his desire for "peaceful coexistence" with the United States. It was a policy scorned by Soviet and Chinese hard-liners, because it implied a major shift of Soviet resources away from the military and aid to allies. Whereas Stalin and old Bolsheviks deemed war against the capitalist world inevitable, Khrushchev insisted that nuclear weapons had made war unwinnable. In fact, he rejected any foreign adventures that risked non-nuclear conflict, because they could easily explode into major war.

But as he turned that sharp ideological corner, Khrushchev had to prove to his associates that he was not abandoning his Marxist-Leninist duty to proletarians around the world. So he argued that concentrating on Soviet economic progress would bring communists "the initiative" in world affairs. And he promised to support anticolonial "wars of national liberation" in places like Vietnam and Algeria. The combination of Soviet domestic progress and the defeat of colonialism abroad, he concluded, would mean that the working class "in time will rule the whole world."

Kennedy failed to grasp the defensive, even isolationist essence of this speech and focused instead on the promised support for "liberation" wars. "One of the most important speeches of the decade," he called it. "Read, mark, learn and inwardly digest," he instructed his foreign policy team. Although Kennedy, too, had opposed the vestiges of French colonialism in Algeria and Vietnam, he was now determined to oppose nationalists who took their inspiration or support from the Soviets and Chinese.

"Let every nation know," he proclaimed in his inaugural the next morning, January 20, "whether it wishes us well or ill, that we shall pay any price, bear any burden, meet any hardship, support any friend, oppose any foe, in order to assure the survival and the success of liberty." He said he would not fear to negotiate with the Soviet Union for a reduction of tensions and weapons, but he went on to predict "a long twilight struggle" against tyranny as well as poverty, disease, and war itself. And in his first days as president, Kennedy moved to increase U.S. military spending by 15 percent, to speed the production of nuclear missiles, and to prepare the army and marines to fight antiguerrilla wars.

KENNEDY'S DESIRE TO ENGAGE the world with a combination of power and prudence led swiftly, however, to a calamity at Cuba's Bay of Pigs. As urged by Eisenhower, he approved the plan of the CIA to land thirteen hundred Cuban exiles on a Cuban shore, with the aim of inspiring a revolution to overthrow Fidel Castro. But the new president wanted also to deny U.S. involvement, to preserve his progressive reputation in Latin America and to avoid provoking Castro's Soviet allies. He therefore withheld even modest air support for the expedition in April 1961, and its utter failure left him looking inept and irresolute. Two months later, he bore these wounds to a Vienna summit meeting with Khrushchev, who promptly rubbed them with a stinging dose of salt.

Kennedy went to persuade Khrushchev to avoid interventions that risked conflict in unsettled and unaligned regions of the world. But the Soviet leader berated him for standing on the "wrong side of history," thinking he could halt the spread of communism with military bases all around Russia. America stood with colonialists and dictators, whereas the Soviet Union supported "holy wars" of national liberation. Cuba was a perfect example, Khrushchev argued; invading that island had only strengthened Fidel's regime. Castro was no communist, but American policy would make him one.

The president sheepishly conceded that invading Cuba had been a mistake. But when he cautioned that Castro must not become a threat to other Latin governments, Khrushchev scoffed again: How could six million Cubans threaten the great United States? Kennedy's pitch for global stability was turned entirely against him. He was made to feel young and inexperienced, a weakling who had lacked the courage even to finish off Castro.

Actually, Khrushchev judged him intelligent and sensitive but, indeed, a touch weak. So the next day, the chairman drove full throttle toward his main objective—the permanent division of Germany and Europe. He announced that he would finally sign that peace treaty with East Germany before the end of the year. He might tolerate a tame, unaligned "free city" of West Berlin, but if Kennedy refused to sign, Berlin would be absorbed in the communist East.

On this issue, however, the president was primed to stand firm. He would risk war to preserve access to Berlin, he said; it was the fruit of victory over the Nazis, not a gift of Moscow. Khrushchev could sign whatever he wanted, but Berlin symbolized America's commitment to the defense of Western Europe. Kennedy emphasized as they parted that conflict in Europe risked mutual destruction. Khrushchev replied that the choice for war was Kennedy's; that German treaty would be signed in December. Well then, the president observed, it will be a cold winter.

Minutes later, at a prearranged interview with James "Scotty" Reston of *The New York Times*, Kennedy conceded that Khrushchev "just beat hell out of me." He would now have to prove his mettle, increasing military spending again and sending troops to resist a communist insurgency in Vietnam. "I think he thought that anyone who was so young and inexperienced as to get into that [Cuban] mess could be taken," Kennedy said, still smarting from his Bay of Pigs failure. "And anyone who got into it and didn't see it through had no guts."

Yet to his aide, Kenneth O'Donnell, Kennedy acknowledged that he was playing a weak hand in Berlin: "If I am going to threaten nuclear war it will have to be for much bigger . . . reasons than that."

K and K were standing toe-to-toe. They could only hope, through their separate vulnerabilities, that they were pitting bluff against bluff.

WE NOW KNOW THAT KHRUSHCHEV'S angry performance at Vienna was propelled by an ill wind at his back. The East German rulers were screaming for help; they could not much longer survive the westward flight of their people through the Berlin escape hatch. And the Soviet military clamored for a larger budget to match the Kennedy buildup and to cope with the tensions Khrushchev had created in Central Europe. From a Soviet perspective, the main problem was not America's weakness or Kennedy's timidity. It was the United States' overwhelming strength.

After Vienna Khrushchev was compelled to cancel a further reduction of the Soviet armed forces by another 1.2 million men and to increase military spending by a third. Kennedy came home and called up 150,000 reserves, enlarged the military draft, and endorsed Defense Secretary McNamara's call for a more "flexible" military that could wage war in Europe without immediately escalating to an all-out nuclear exchange.

Then in August 1961, Khrushchev let the East Germans run a barbed-wire fence clear through the middle of Berlin to end the flights of refugees. When Kennedy failed to challenge the wire, it was quickly supplanted by brick. As I discovered for one of my first diplomatic reports from Washington, the White House squeals of protest against this infamous wall were only meant to dramatize communist failure. The president actually favored a more stable East Germany; he did not want a rebellion there tempting the West Germans to intervene and drawing the superpowers into conflict. Kennedy also found relief in the thought that Khrushchev would not now challenge Western access to Berlin; why bear the stigma of that ugly wall if he still intended to seize the entire city?

THERE COULD BE NO LASTING RELIEF, however, so long as the superpowers struggled to impress each other with their missile prowess. Nuclear weapons were usable only if one side could devastate the opponent's entire force in a "first strike." If each possessed a survivable "second strike" capacity, then nuclear weapons served only to deter war, not to wage it. Then again, if one side's weapons and cities were securely defended, might it not be tempted to mount a preemptive attack?

Kennedy and Khrushchev were the first leaders to confront these circular theories and vulnerabilities. And they could not shed the habit of speaking about, and seeking, military "security" and "superiority." The arms race raged on, propelled by the fears of surprise attack, of being underrated or judged unwilling to push the nuclear button.

Kennedy exploited nuclear fears in his campaign for the White House, complaining that Eisenhower had risked a "missile gap" in Russia's favor. But there was no gap when Kennedy took the oath. By August 1961, American satellites estimated from ninety miles up that the Russians possessed not 150 to 200 intercontinental missiles, as previously thought, but a mere two dozen clumsy models. The United States enjoyed a lead of at least five to one in ICBMs as well as a superior force of bombers and brand new medium-range missiles aboard well-hidden submarines.[5] Kennedy may have felt weak, but he was overwhelmingly the stronger. Khrushchev talked big, but knew that he faced a long period of inferiority. They were equal only in the need to impress each other, and that need propelled them inexorably toward the crisis over Cuba.

The Soviets kept claiming strategic "equality," which caused Kennedy to be accused at home of failing to impress them with America's strength and mettle. So in mid-October 1961, the president drew attention to the great increases he had ordered in both nuclear and conventional forces. Khrushchev answered with a shocking announcement that, contrary to his promise at Vienna, he was breaking a voluntary, three-year moratorium on radiation-spewing nuclear tests. He began by exploding a fifty-megaton thermonuclear device, the largest ever. Behind that cloud, he appeased his anxious generals by again canceling the peace treaty signing promised for December.

Kennedy now felt compelled to impress Khrushchev as well as domestic critics with a detailed inventory of American nuclear might. Together with McNamara, Rusk, and Bundy, the president wrote a reassuring speech to be delivered sotto voce by Roswell Gilpatric, the deputy secretary of defense. But the speech was hardly subtle. It described an arsenal of "tens of thousands" of tactical and strategic delivery vehicles poised to strike at Soviet targets from the air, land, and sea, from bases near and far—and "of course" more than one nuclear warhead for each vehicle. These forces were so deployed that no sneak attack could effectively disarm the United States. "In short, we have a second-strike capability which is at least as extensive as what the Soviets can deliver by striking first. Therefore we are confident that the Soviets will not provoke a major nuclear conflict."

---

[5] Later intelligence showed an even greater margin since some Soviet ICBMs were dummy decoys and "demonstration" models.

News of the Gilpatric speech reached Moscow when it hurt the most, during a contentious meeting of world communist leaders from which China's Premier Zhou Enlai had just walked out, disdaining Khrushchev's timid leadership. Ordered to answer Gilpatric—and the Chinese—Marshal Malinovsky dismissed the American nuclear arithmetic. Just a few huge warheads, which he could deliver to any spot on earth, were sufficient to deter the "madmen" hatching plans against the Soviet Union. "What is there to say to this petty speech? Only one thing: The threat does not frighten us!"

But Washington refused to relent. In the same week, Rusk said the two nations were militarily equal "only" in their ability to inflict great damage; they were decidedly unequal in total power. McNamara piled on by claiming a nuclear force several times greater than that of the Soviets. And when asked about all the boasts, Kennedy said with a smile that he would not want to trade places with anyone. Still, to appease a Congress aroused by the Soviet nuclear tests, Kennedy crowded Khrushchev further by ordering many more ICBMs than his own strategists deemed necessary. The chairman answered lamely that his "100-megaton bombs" made it "impossible to intimidate us."

The backstage relationship of the two leaders was a tad less contentious. They had begun a secret correspondence to debate their differences about Central Europe and Southeast Asia. One such exchange actually helped to dissolve a confrontation of their tanks in Berlin after East Germans questioned an American diplomat's access to their half of the city. The secret letters were augmented by cordial contacts between Robert Kennedy and Georgi Bolshakov, a high-level Soviet agent in Washington, who sometimes brought oral messages from Khrushchev. But the tensions persisted into early 1962, when Kennedy felt that he, too, had to resume open-air testing to improve his nuclear weapons. Khrushchev took this as an affront by a president who had loudly claimed strategic superiority, and suffered a further political defeat at home. His central committee blocked the transfer of funds from the military to agriculture, forcing Khrushchev to raise food prices, inviting new protest riots.

The mutual baiting did not end. Trying to explain his plans for a "flexible" response to an attack on Berlin, Kennedy said during a magazine interview in March that "in some circumstances we might have to take the initiative." The writer, his friend Stewart Alsop, rightly interpreted this as a retreat from the policy of never being the first to fire nuclear weapons. Soviet propagandists seized on the remark as a threat of preemptive war, but even correctly read, the specter of a first strike amounted to a further public challenge of Khrushchev's military posture. And it was published only weeks after Soviet rocket designers had informed Khrushchev of the poor prospects for their long-range missiles.

Their first ICBMs, called R-7s, had proved too costly to maintain. They required a factory for refitting components at every launch site; for a semblance of accuracy, they also needed to be steered from two radio guidance points three hundred miles apart along the flight path. A better, cheaper R-16 design had been chosen in 1959 but, unlike the American Minuteman, it needed to be fueled for several hours before launch to prevent corrosion. As one designer observed, "nothing would be left of us" by the time it was fired. An alternative team, working on the R-9, had encountered still more difficulty. Moreover, Soviet missile units, lacking good reconnaissance, had only approximate coordinates for the American targets they might want to hit. As Sergei Khrushchev recalled, "When he brandished missiles, father had no idea that the military simply didn't know where to shoot." America's Minuteman ICBMs were rolling off assembly lines. A comparable Soviet force was years away.

As always in his seasons of discontent, Khrushchev pined for a bold stroke that might reverse his fortunes, a wily end run around his predicament, a bold surprise for allies and adversaries alike. By the time Kennedy's press secretary, Pierre Salinger, visited Moscow in early May 1962, Khrushchev had dreamed up his "Hail Mary" missile pass to Cuba and could not resist a hint of it. He said Kennedy's warning, that he might be the first to use a nuclear bomb, had been "a very bad mistake—for which he will have to pay." Khrushchev did not, however, mention Cuba, the chosen site for his payback.

FIVE

THE THORN IN THE FLESH

A FEW DOZEN NUCLEAR MISSILES IN CUBA IN 1962 MAY OR may not have posed a serious military challenge to the United States. The degree of danger was debated then, and long after. But Fidel Castro needed no missiles to frighten Washington. His resentment of American domination and his embrace of Soviet ideology inspired radicals the world over, and especially in Latin America, where military juntas ruled in the service of U.S. corporate interests. Castro fed on *Yanqui* hatred because Americans behaved as if they owned Cuba. Which before him they did.[6]

It was to "liberate" Cuba that the United States first went to war against Spain in 1898 in an imperial spasm that also grabbed Puerto Rico, plus the Philippines and Guam half a world away. Cubans had worn down their Spanish masters in three decades of intermittent

---

[6] Cubans also fiercely resent the USA calling itself "America," as if we are the only Americans. Their polite term for us is *norteamericanos*—never mind the implication for Canadians. But Yankee habit has led me to use *America* and its variants as convenient synonyms for "United States."

guerrilla warfare, but they succeeded only in becoming a protectorate of the United States. Sugar plantations and refineries, railroads and utilities passed into American hands. And when they bargained for a measure of self-government in 1902, Cubans were forced to accept the notorious Platt Amendment, which gave the United States the right to intervene with troops on virtually any pretext. Many Americans thought at the time they were actively preparing Cuba for annexation and statehood.

American troops returned to Cuba in 1906 to deal with political unrest and again in 1912 to break up a protest by black Cubans against discrimination. President Wilson sent in the marines in World War I, to assure Cuba's help in defending the Caribbean and Panama Canal, and they stayed for five years to secure America's domination of the island's booming sugar economy. President Franklin D. Roosevelt renounced the Platt Amendment in the 1930s for the sake of a "good neighbor" approach to Latin America, but this did not much diminish the giant neighbor's dominion. Although Cubans practiced a lively, sometimes even radical politics, they failed to sustain any challenge to the authority of the United States and its economic barons. Little was done to relieve the frustrations of the great majority of poor, illiterate workers and peasants, causing much labor strife and violent displays of sympathy from student radicals.

It was in this cauldron of university politics in the late 1940s and early 1950s, as colorfully depicted by my late colleague, Tad Szulc,[7] that Fidel Castro discovered his passion for revolution. He acquired a yearning for Cuban independence, a flair for charismatic oratory, and a gift for manipulating political allies. He set out to emulate the life of the martyred José Martí, a brilliant nineteenth-century poet and polemicist who preached social revolution and led the last struggles against Spain. But in Castro's reiteration of Martí's doctrines, American imperialism replaced Spain's as the obstacle to social upheaval and Cuba's self-assertion.

---

[7] Szulc, Tad. *Fidel: A Critical Portrait*. New York: William Morrow, 1986.

In these same decades, bracketing World War II, a former army sergeant named Fulgencio Batista became Castro's perfect foil. Alternating alliance with the left and right, Batista was elected as a reformist president in 1940, then lost and moved to Florida, returned in 1949, and led a coup in 1952 that produced a corrupt, repressive regime. He came to embody the twin evils of tyranny and Yankee exploitation, offending almost all Cubans. Even conservative Americans celebrated his downfall—taken in, like many Cubans, by Castro's promise of democracy.

Although he tried to hide it, Fidel Castro was born in 1926 into a family of affluent landowners. He attended an elite Jesuit boarding school, where he emerged as a superb athlete and brilliant but, he claims, irreligious student. At nineteen, he enrolled in the law faculty of Havana University, already feeling himself a leader among boys. But only now, in the protected arena of campus politics—no police allowed!—did he develop muscular views, ambitions, and organizing skills. By age twenty-six, a lawyer and vaguely socialist, he was close to winning a seat in Congress when Batista's coup intervened. Almost overnight, the candidate became a conspirator, leading a bloody but futile quest for weapons by attacking an army barrack in Santiago on July 26, 1953. At trial, Castro delivered a peroration that made him famous; he polished the words in prison and had them disseminated by supporters to cast himself as the leader of all resistance to Batista: "I know that imprisonment will be harder for me than it has ever been for anyone, filled with cowardly threats and hideous cruelty. But I do not fear prison, as I do not fear the fury of the miserable tyrant who took the lives of 70 of my comrades. Condemn me. It does not matter. *History will absolve me.*"[8]

---

[8] Castro's prophecy of absolution paraphrased—knowingly, it seems—another fiery prediction from captivity: "And the statesmen who will have decreed this sacrifice may be persecuted by their contemporaries, but posterity will absolve them from all guilt for having demanded this offering from their people."—*Mein Kampf,* by Adolf Hitler, volume 2, chapter 14.

Prison may have been hard, but it was also brief. Sentenced to fifteen years, Castro was freed in a general amnesty in 1955, two years after the botched attack. He and his brother, Raúl, fled to Mexico where, with a radical physician from Argentina, Ernesto "Che" Guevara, they prepared to invade Cuba and wage a guerrilla war in alliance with an urban underground. They named themselves the 26th of July Movement, not to celebrate Castro's first failure but to stake a claim to chronological precedence among the many anti-Batista factions.

I BRIEFLY COVERED THE TRIUMPHANT Fidel when assigned by *The Times* to look past his bizarre conduct, guerrilla uniform, and demagogic oratory to discover his true political convictions. Castro's three- and four-hour harangues had confused Americans about his ideology; in fact, reporters were often asked whether he was fundamentally crazy. My answer: no more crazy than anyone who set out with a boatload of eighty-two men to conquer a nation of six million.

The truth was stranger still, because only about twenty of those men survived a mistimed landing and disastrous ambush when they reached the island in December 1956. The Castro brothers were forced to reinvent their guerrilla strategy while hiding in the mountains of eastern Cuba. They emerged victorious two years later because of mass defections from a rotting Batista army. And they easily prevailed over other rebellious groups in what had become a political vacuum. Even Cuba's Communist party was compromised by its former collaboration with Batista and its early disdain for the bearded Fidelistas in the hills.

Castro proclaimed himself the indisputable *commandante* of the resistance, rural and urban. But since his army never exceeded three thousand men, he needed allies to seize power across the island. The most loyal recruits were found by Raúl and Che among their soul mates in the underground of radical young communists. Fidel himself enjoyed broader appeal; he promised a democratic constitution, free elections, and civil liberties, an essentially centrist program except for a far-reaching land reform to mobilize the peasantry. The imperatives of command, however, kept dragging him leftward as he marched toward Havana, alienating the more democratic, less anti-American branches of the movement. Just weeks before Batista finally fled the island, Castro survived a challenge from urban moderates and gave preeminence to the Marxists in his ranks, led by Raúl and Che.

When it came time to govern Cuba, starting on New Year's Day, 1959, Fidel had an even greater need for the organized cadres of the left, including the now repentant communists. Under the rubric of "agrarian reform," he created a secret hierarchy of officials who gradually replaced his centrist ministers. And he summoned street rallies to shout approval for his radical edicts. With overbearing but brilliant orations, Castro evoked cheers for the mass executions of Batista's henchmen and assorted "counter-revolutionaries." He celebrated the flight to Miami of the dispossessed upper classes. He held out visions of plenty, equality, literacy, dignity, and relief from American "imperialism." The assent of the crowds, he argued, was the only "election" he needed. Constitutions were superfluous; too often they only shielded tyrannies. Besides, he finally acknowledged, genuine revolutions have to be decreed rather than voted into being.

Castro masterfully paced Cuba's conversion from Catholicism to communism. He even understood the need to restrain his hostility against the United States until he could secure other sources of trade, aid, and weapons.

AT FIRST, MANY AMERICANS looked upon Castro with a fascinated agnosticism. He came north in April 1959 to reassure nervous investors, to charm campus romantics, and to deflect the suspicions of the Eisenhower administration. Yet even as Fidel met with Vice President Richard Nixon, who judged him to be a budding communist,

brother Raúl was sending aides to Moscow to solicit arms from communist arsenals. Some Soviet officials were afraid that aiding Cuba's
revolution risked American action against Castro, but Khrushchev
loved dipping his toe in Latin waters; that, he boasted to his hard-line
critics, was something Stalin could never accomplish.

By October, Raúl Castro came out of the shadows to take charge
of the Cuban army and police. Fidelistas who refused to serve under
his communist cabal fled into exile or, like Fidel's once close friend,
Húber Matos, were packed off to jail. When Aleksandr Alekseyev, the
Spanish-speaking star of Soviet intelligence, reached Havana to court
the Cuban leaders in the guise of a journalist, Castro confided that he
was waiting for hostile American actions to help sell the Cuban public on closer ties to the Kremlin.

The inevitable hostilities erupted soon enough. Castro's vision of
independence could not sustain cordial relations with the capitalist
colossus to the north. And America's sway in hemisphere affairs could
not tolerate a beacon of revolution aimed at Latin America. As Castro
told Szulc a quarter century later: "I do not pretend that [American]
aggressions are the cause of socialism [that is, communism] in Cuba.
This is false. In Cuba we were going to construct socialism in the
most orderly possible manner, within a reasonable period of time,
with the least amount of trauma and problems, but the aggressions of
imperialism accelerated the revolutionary process."

Plots to overthrow Castro were not officially contemplated in
Washington until early 1960, but they were discussed in intelligence
circles throughout 1959, especially at the CIA, which had proudly
overthrown leftist leaders in the Congo, Iran, and Guatemala. And
communists were obviously replacing even loyal Fidelistas in the
summer of 1959, taking charge of Cuban towns and villages and
major government departments. Castro himself staged a cynical "res-
ignation" as premier to accelerate the purge of the moderate he had
named president of Cuba and to incite the crowds to beg for his
own return. By the time the first prominent Soviet leader, Anastas

Mikoyan, visited Havana in February 1960, Cuba's relationship with the United States was already irreparable.

"Yes, he is a genuine revolutionary—completely like us," Mikoyan reported to Khrushchev. "I felt as though I had returned to my childhood!" The Russians were impressed by Fidel's revolutionary ardor and overjoyed to see communism planted on America's doorstep without the intervention, as in Europe, of the Soviet army. Mikoyan agreed to buy a fifth of Cuba's sugar crop at bargain prices in exchange for Soviet oil and other barter. When, just three weeks later, a French freighter bearing munitions from Western Europe exploded in Havana harbor, the Castro brothers found cause—or pretext—to call it American sabotage and quickly begged for still more Soviet support. The cause of the explosion, which killed nearly a hundred people, was never determined, but it coincided with Eisenhower's secret approval of plans to dislodge Castro at the end of 1960, with an invasion of exiles and various assassination schemes.

By May 1960, Havana and Moscow established formal diplomatic relations while the CIA began anti-Castro broadcasts to Cuba. In June, Raúl was received in Moscow and promised tanks and one hundred thousand rifles. The first Soviet oil arrived in Cuba and when Americans refused to process it, Castro seized their refineries. Khrushchev, conscious of Chinese taunts that he was neglecting his international duties, vowed expansively to protect Cuba from afar: "The Soviet Union does not need bases for missiles in Cuba for it is enough to press a button here to launch missiles to any part of the world." But he said later that he was speaking only "figuratively."

Eisenhower canceled most sugar imports from Cuba in July, and Khrushchev took up the slack. In August, the CIA urged the Mafia to kill Castro and, incidentally, rescue the mob's gambling enterprises in Havana. And the KGB changed its code name for Cuba operations from *yuntsie*, meaning "young ones," to *avanpost*, meaning "outpost" or "beachhead."

. . .

AFTER MY SERVICE IN KHRUSHCHEV'S Moscow for three years, *The Times* assigned me to Havana in 1960 to resolve a question still debated by Americans: Was Castro a communist or merely the bane of exploiting capitalists? I began this investigation in New York in September, watching Fidel and Khrushchev embrace on a Harlem sidewalk at the start of a pointless gathering of world leaders at the United Nations. Castro took up residence in the black community to dramatize the inhospitality of American innkeepers; his threat to pitch a tent in Central Park had produced an appealing invitation from the Hotel Theresa on 125th Street. Never a man to be outdone in self-advertisements, Khrushchev's first outing in Manhattan became a visit to Fidel.

Castro received me at the Theresa at the urging of Herbert Matthews, to whom he was deeply obligated. A *Times* correspondent and editorial writer, Matthews had been smuggled into Castro's mountain hideout to interview Fidel in early 1957, after Batista declared him dead. The news that he was alive landed explosively on front pages everywhere. Moreover, Matthews was fooled into exaggerating the size of Castro's guerrilla force and had vouchsafed his claims to be a freedom-loving democrat. My first question to Castro when introduced by Matthews in the Theresa Café produced an uninterruptible oration as well as an empty promise that we would meet again soon when I reached Havana.

On his return home in October 1960, Castro formally seized about a billion dollars' worth of American investments with only vague talk of one day paying compensation. The United States responded with an embargo on all sales to Cuba, except for food and medicines. October was when Vice President Nixon had wanted the CIA to unleash the exiles it was training to invade Cuba, figuring that their success would assure his election to the White House. Kennedy, his opponent, feared just such an "October surprise," so he outbid Nixon and *publicly* urged action by Cuban "freedom fighters." The enraged vice president redoubled the cynicism by condemning Kennedy for suggesting an "irresponsible" intervention. Whereupon Kennedy argued—truthfully at last, and fatefully as it would develop—that he meant only to express "sympathy" for the exiles; he said he opposed American "involvement" in any invasion.

In Havana, meanwhile, the growing fears of attack caused the Castro regime to stress that Soviet missiles would punish any attack, whereupon Khrushchev, hoping for warmer relations with the next American president, emphasized that he wanted his rocket rattling to remain "symbolic." My report about this Soviet counsel of restraint angered leading Cubans, but it also led to a long interview with the cleverest of Cuba's communists. The charming Carlos Rafael Rodríguez, who eventually became president of Cuba, candidly answered the question my editors had posed. Speaking as Castro's ideological tutor, he said Fidel's slow but certain mastery of Marxism had made an overt communist seizure of power unnecessary. He spoke the truth, but in cold print the report might have been used to justify America's armed intervention, so Rodríguez denounced me as a liar and ended my Havana career.

When Eisenhower, in his last days as president, broke diplomatic relations, Cuba began to require visas for visitors. My application was promptly denied, and I returned to the island only once more, in April 1961, to the American naval base at Guantánamo, where I could monitor Cuban television during the new president's calamitous adventure at the Bay of Pigs.

JOHN KENNEDY UNDERSTOOD the sources of revolution in poor countries. As a senator, he often deplored colonialism—especially the French variety in Algiers. And he sympathized with the Cubans who resented American ownership of half their sugar lands and almost all cattle ranches, mines, oil refineries, and utilities. He recognized economic injustice in much of Latin America and intended as president to outbid Fidel Castro with an "Alliance for Progress" that would increase aid to the more enlightened hemisphere regimes.

But the Kennedy family's friends in Palm Beach undermined those sympathies. They regarded Castro as a communist before Fidel confessed his attraction; he was despoiling their Cuban playground and seizing their friends' properties. Besides, at the height of the Cold War, no Democrat could afford to "lose" more territory to regimes aligned with the Soviet Union, especially not territory so close to our shore. And that was doubly true for a Democrat elected president by just a hair.

On meeting his successor, Eisenhower told Kennedy he must not allow the Castro government to survive. When Kennedy asked whether he should support the Cuban exiles then being trained, no longer so secretly, by the CIA in Guatemala, Ike replied, "to the utmost." But Kennedy feared accepting this advice as much as he feared ignoring it. He wanted to be rid of Castro, but he also wanted to tempt the Soviets into arms control negotiations and accommodations the world over. He did not want to begin his reign with acts of aggression, but he could not bring himself to accept Senator J. William Fulbright's sound advice to simply ignore Castro, to treat him as "a thorn in the flesh, not a dagger to the heart."

So the novice president altered the CIA's invasion plans. He would withhold all overt support so that he could lie about America's covert involvement in the plot. He trusted the assurances of Eisenhower operatives that an exile beachhead on Cuban soil would be enough to proclaim a legitimate anti-Castro government and foment a popular uprising. Publicly, Kennedy insisted clear up to D-day that Cubans alone would decide their future without American interference. Accordingly, after the first sorties of unmarked old American bombers failed to destroy all of Castro's tiny air force, Kennedy canceled further flights and left the invaders to Castro's mercy, stranded on the beach at the Bay of Pigs. Only 14 were rescued; 107 were killed, and 1,189 were taken prisoner.

The victory emboldened Castro to declare, in the jargon of the Soviet Union, that Cuba was now a "socialist"—meaning communist—state. He openly invited hundreds of Soviet technicians and "security specialists" to help him arrest tens of thousands of Cuban "counter-revolutionaries." He exploited the attack to solicit more weapons from communist countries and to bring nationalist passions in Cuba to a boil.

Sympathy for a humiliated president momentarily increased Kennedy's standing with the American public, but contempt for his vacillation was soon heard even from Moscow. With the exiles already routed, Khrushchev gratuitously warned of a catastrophic chain reaction because he intended to give Cuba "all necessary help." He was delighted to claim that his rocket rattling had defeated American aggression and that Soviet support was now the "decisive factor" in world affairs.

Kennedy replied meekly that he would not be lectured "by those who bloodied the streets of Budapest." And indeed, since Khrushchev did not want the United States to crush the Cubans as he had crushed the Hungarians, the chairman momentarily stopped taunting the wounded president. "Our government does not seek any advantages or privileges in Cuba," he wrote. "We have no bases in Cuba and we do not intend to establish any."

Still, Kennedy was haunted by the failure, particularly after Khrushchev's rude treatment of him in their Vienna meetings. The president became desperate to regain his footing, to demonstrate resolve. And his brother, who had played no significant role in the Bay of Pigs misadventure, now spewed fire in all directions. Bobby wanted the misguided advisers purged from the CIA and Pentagon. He demanded secret action to overthrow Castro. And he took no comfort from Khrushchev's reassurances. "If we don't want Russia to set up

missile bases in Cuba," he warned prophetically, "we had better decide now what we are willing to do to stop it."

After toying with the idea of making his brother head of the CIA,
Kennedy chose the politically safer course of naming another Republican and Eisenhower intimate, John McCone, to replace Allen
Dulles. But Attorney General Robert Kennedy seized command of
the planning to undermine Castro, whose downfall he proclaimed to
be the administration's "top priority." More assassination schemes
were sanctioned, as were covert attacks on Cuban ships and factories
to incite rebellion. At one point, Robert Kennedy even considered
staging provocations, perhaps an attack on the Guantánamo naval
base, to justify a direct American invasion. As Defense Secretary Mc-
Namara recalled, "we were hysterical about Castro," under constant
pressure from the Kennedy brothers to get rid of him.

All the anti-Castro exertions have never been fully documented.
The best records deal with "Operation Mongoose," a plan hatched by
a guerrilla fighter of mixed reputation, Brigadier General Edward
Lansdale, a Kennedy favorite for a time. His plan envisioned wide-
spread sabotage and the infiltration of agents and guerrilla fighters to
inspire a rebellion that could become the pretext for American military
intervention by October 1962. But the CIA and Pentagon dragged
their feet; the plan produced a few pinpricks that only stiffened Castro's
defenses and buttressed his requests for more Soviet arms.

Various other schemes to discredit or kill Castro produced no
known close calls. There were efforts to dope him with chemicals,
to spike his cigars with drugs, to poison his wet suit or fountain
pens, to sneak a depilatory agent into his shoes to make his beard fall
out. Robert Kennedy's pressure to act was described by Richard
Helms, a McCone deputy at the CIA, as "white heat." But McCone
always insisted that he opposed the contacts with the underworld to
arrange for hired assassins. Most officials eventually concluded that
Castro could be overthrown only with a direct military invasion,
which President Kennedy refused to authorize. He so advised

Khrushchev's son-in-law in private conversation even as he compared his proprietary feelings about Cuba to Soviet feelings about Hungary. And with this comparison, the president inadvertently heightened concerns in Moscow and Havana that he did, after all, plan to follow Khrushchev's example in Hungary with another attack on Cuba—this time effective.

The best evidence suggests that Kennedy hoped to destroy the Castro regime from afar, invading the island only after Fidel had been toppled from within. But with Castro now proclaiming himself a Marxist-Leninist "until the last day of my life," the president had to refute Republican charges that he was acquiescing in the spread of communism to the hemisphere. In early 1962, Kennedy halted all U.S. trade with Cuba and lobbied other nations to join the boycott. He arranged for Cuba's exclusion from the Organization of American States. And he ordered the Pentagon to prepare assorted contingency plans for striking at Cuba, with a naval blockade, air attacks, troop landings, or some combination of all three. In April, just as Khrushchev finally agreed to honor Castro's six-month-old request for antiaircraft missiles and other defensive weapons, Kennedy took the shah of Iran to witness naval maneuvers that were conspicuous rehearsals for an island landing by forty thousand U.S. troops. And half a year later, on October 15, just hours before the White House discovered offensive missiles in Cuba, the Pentagon undertook a major amphibious exercise in the Caribbean aimed at the overthrow of the hard-to-mistake "ORTSAC," an exercise designed to impress American voters no less than the Russians.

As McNamara and others later acknowledged, Cubans watching all this muscle flexing had every right to conclude that they were targeted for attack and that Kennedy did not intend to fail a second time. Castro prepared elaborate defenses, organizing a militia of 250,000 to back up his army of 50,000. If he could not deter an invasion, he obviously planned to wage unending guerrilla war against an American occupation.

Yet Kennedy's top aides always maintained that the president had no intention of invading Cuba and risking a guerrilla conflict. They respected the Castro forces and estimated that an invasion would cost twenty thousand American casualties. Consistent and credible denials that an invasion was ever planned have come from McNamara, who controlled all American military forces, as well as from Robert Kennedy and ranking White House advisers like McGeorge Bundy and Theodore Sorensen. In the words of Edwin Martin, the assistant secretary of state for Latin America, who oversaw Cuban affairs and sat prominently among Kennedy's managers of the Missile Crisis, the defined U.S. policy before October 1962 was to damage the Cuban economy with boycotts, infiltration, and sabotage; to raise the cost of Soviet support for Castro; and to prevent the spread of Cuban and Soviet influence in Latin America. No less, but no more.

Further evidence came from Kennedy himself. Five days before he learned of the Soviet missile bases in Cuba, the president arranged a special briefing for my boss in Washington, Scotty Reston, to deflect Republican demands for action against Castro. Concluding his *New York Times* column on October 12, 1962, without naming his White House sources, Reston wrote: "In present circumstances, there will be no invasion and no blockade and no acquiescence in Soviet control of Cuba. But there will be total surveillance of Cuba and there will be more turmoil in Cuba than Castro has yet experienced or imagined."

And that is how Soviet intelligence, too, read Kennedy's intentions in the fall of 1962. While Khrushchev had argued to his colleagues and to Castro that only nuclear missiles in Cuba could deter an American assault, he actually trusted his analysts' judgment that Kennedy would wage only economic warfare against the island. By October 15, he considered the Cuban bases virtually finished and a diplomatic fait accompli that Kennedy would have to swallow. Speaking with the president of Finland, Urho Kekkonen, Khrushchev said he "now" thought Cuba was safe from U.S. attack.

But Khrushchev's defense minister, Marshal Malinovsky, was getting nervous about construction delays in Cuba and bad omens elsewhere. That same October day, responding to American objections to the unusual number of Soviet flights to Cuba, the government of Guinea halted the refueling of Russian aircraft. A Soviet inspection party led by General Anatoly Gribkov, who had led the planning for Operation Anadyr, was forced to land instead in Dakar, Senegal, where they also felt unwelcome. The Russians each had a per-diem allowance of only ten dollars, but after sunbathing on the beach, it cost each of them six dollars to reclaim their clothes from a suddenly enterprising hotel dry cleaner. After some overnight haggling about expenses, their plane was allowed to continue to Havana. But their luggage wound up back in Moscow, where its arrival, Gribkov recalled, caused several military wives to faint. They imagined, prophetically, that the Soviet expedition to Cuba had met with a terrible fate.

SIX

THE ROCKETS HIT HOME

JOHN KENNEDY HAD NO DOUBT ABOUT THE TARGET OF Khrushchev's missiles. "He can't do that to me!" was his first reaction. The moment he saw those photos of scratched earth and ominous tubes in western Cuba, on Tuesday morning, October 16, he felt himself threatened even more than the nation. The United States was well enough armed to meet any Soviet military challenge. But was the president?

Khrushchev must really think him spineless, Kennedy decided. That's what Robert Frost, the poet, had reported to him after a recent visit to the chairman's vacation home. Kennedy's fear of being judged irresolute had festered for more than a year, ever since the Bay of Pigs. Now it became a presidential pronouncement: "He can't do that—to *me*!"

But what was Khrushchev actually doing? A few Soviet missiles in Cuba were no different from some American missiles in Turkey, or Italy, or Britain, or beneath the sea in submarines. Missile bases in friendly countries did not violate any law or even custom. The Russians were only doing what the Americans had done. And while they did it secretly, modern spy planes and satellites would have found them out soon enough. Besides, the missiles were not there to be fired; they were meant to intimidate, to retaliate if necessary, and mainly to negotiate with enhanced prestige and confidence. Negotiate for what? Khrushchev was still maneuvering for Berlin and that German peace treaty, Kennedy figured.

But Khrushchev had daringly deceived him, Kennedy realized. Not just deceived, actually lied. Even his secret, private letters were sent to mislead. So were the sly messages delivered by Soviet agents and diplomats. The lies, Kennedy concluded, were more dangerous than the missiles. Without some minimal trust between the two men who walked and slept beside the nuclear button, there was little chance of restraining the Soviet–American rivalry, cooling confrontations, and averting a war that neither could possibly want. Unless challenged, the president thought, Khrushchev might run even more dangerous risks for strategic advantage. The stakes here were not the future of Cuba and Latin America, or even the freedom of Berlin or the cohesion of the Western alliance. Being tested was the leader of the West, and the fate of his presidency. That was the ultimate stake: the political danger at home now that events had vindicated the Republican demagogues clamoring for action against the Soviet buildup in Cuba. He would be remembered in history, the president remarked to Ken O'Donnell, for "looking away" while Khrushchev blindsided him ninety miles off the Florida coast. He just could not—would not—let him get away with it.

Did the missiles themselves pose such a great threat that their removal justified a risk of war? Even a world war, fought with nuclear weapons? As Kennedy's national security adviser, McGeorge Bundy, recalled the mood around the White House that week, "What we perceived was more an intolerable affront than an unacceptable attempt to change the nuclear balance of power." Hostile missiles so close to home inflamed the psyche of Americans. Khrushchev's missile threats from afar were challenge enough, but the missiles in Cuba had leapt across our ocean moats. They were intolerable psychologically and geographically, and also diplomatically if they fueled a new Soviet militancy on issues like Berlin. They might even become dangerous militarily, if over time the Russians expanded and improved their Cuban arsenal.

For now, however, the greatest offense was Khrushchev's deception. It made Kennedy appear not just weak but also dangerously gullible. With controlled yet obvious anger, the president summoned his top aides to consider his options. He did not really want advice about what to do. Those lies were going to be punished. Those missiles were going to be removed. The only question was how.

KHRUSHCHEV HAD HOPED to shock him by surprise and Kennedy resolved to pay him back in kind. He ordered rigorous surveillance of Cuba by U-2 spy planes to count the missiles and track their installation. But he also demanded strict secrecy about discovery of the missiles. He wanted nothing said or done to rob him of the benefit of surprise once he decided on a course of action. Secrecy would shift the initiative in this crisis from the Kremlin to the White House.

The team that Kennedy summoned to analyze the situation, therefore, was an informal, even disorderly group of relevant cabinet officers, their top deputies, and a few expert advisers. They met in secret for what turned out to be a week of ad hoc consultation, with no formal agenda or presiding officer. To hide their deliberations, Kennedy and his secretaries of state and defense kept most of their public appointments as if nothing had happened, moving in and out of the conferences. But not even the presence of the president gave the meetings structure; they became a babble of digressions and interruptions, with little regard for rank or responsibility. Between meetings, team members also conferred informally, in smaller groups, but without the benefit of research staffs or secretaries. Not until a week had passed and his options were clear in his mind did Kennedy give the group a formal designation and legal sanction to carry out his instructions. He called it the Executive Committee of the National Security Council, or ExCom, which it has been called ever since.

When the group assembled around the White House cabinet table, Kennedy usually flicked on the hidden microphones that only his secretary and perhaps Robert Kennedy knew about. The resulting tapes produced a fascinating record of some of the crisis planning, and scholars have feasted on the transcripts as they were published in recent years.[9] But readers of this record have to supply their own interpretations of the discussions. They have to learn to separate offhand comments from reasoned proposals. They have to sift through the shifting opinions often offered by the same individual. They must recognize the group dynamic at different moments and also the individual posturing, most notably by the president himself; he was not above disguising his thoughts and fears. Moment to moment, Kennedy would shift from puzzled inquiry to firm command, all the while addressing, or ignoring, random interruptions, some serious, some trivial. He used the group to test his instincts. But most often he nudged the discussion toward consensus and endorsement of the actions he came to favor.

In the first hours of deliberation, the shocked president was inclined to attack the Soviet missiles from the air. But he could not decide whether to give Khrushchev—and maybe Castro—advance notice. If told that their secret was discovered, wouldn't the Soviets

---

[9] My accounts of the recorded ExCom meetings are based on superb transcriptions supervised by Timothy Naftali, Philip Zelikow, and Ernest May and published in three volumes as *The Presidential Recordings: John F. Kennedy.* Philip Zelikow and Ernest May, general editors. New York: W. W. Norton, 2001.

threaten a dire response to any attack, or preemptively strike where they were stronger, against Berlin or American bases in Turkey? Yet an attack without warning against the Soviet bases was bound to kill Russians manning the missile sites, and that, too, risked an escalating conflict. So the president's impulse to attack was quickly cooled by concern for the consequences and a hope that Khrushchev might still be persuaded to retreat.

The first faint pitch for negotiation came in Secretary of State Dean Rusk's opening response to the president's evident desire to attack. A lifelong good soldier, Rusk deemed it his duty to translate Kennedy's objectives into diplomatic deals. He came to the first meeting after conferring with his Soviet experts and subtly injected their counsel of caution into a resolute proposition. "We have an obligation," he said, "to do what has to be done—but to do it in a way that gives everybody a chance to pull away from it before it gets too hard."

The first words from Defense Secretary Robert McNamara shuttled between the two sides of his personality, his innate horror of war and his prideful command of the world's greatest military machine. He delivered the news that the Joint Chiefs of Staff were opposed to any delay for negotiation; they wanted to attack before the Soviet missiles could fire back at the United States. And they were opposed to bombing only missile bases; that would leave some of the missiles undamaged or even undiscovered and expose American pilots to anti-aircraft fire and fighter planes. The chiefs wanted to hit all Soviet and Cuban planes, airfields, guns, and nuclear storage sites, then erect a naval blockade to prevent new weapon deliveries and finish the job with a full-scale invasion. Only General Maxwell Taylor, their chairman and a Kennedy favorite, had some doubt about an invasion. He favored air attacks but feared that an invasion would bog Americans down "in that deep mud in Cuba," meaning a guerrilla war.

The president did not like what he heard from the Pentagon. He kept hoping for a way to conduct only a "surgical" strike at the three known missile sites. He would then send a quick message to Khrushchev that the Soviet deception had been duly answered and that the shooting could now stop. But were there only three missile sites? And what, someone wondered, if an American attack inspired an uprising in Cuba—would that require an invasion to prevent the slaughter of Castro's opponents?

As for the massive bombing urged by the chiefs, it made the Kennedy brothers cringe. Robert Kennedy argued that it would kill a lot of people, offend world opinion, and make it "almost incumbent upon the Russians then to say, 'Well, we're going to send them in again. And if you [bomb] again, we're going to do the same thing to Turkey.'" Behind that reluctance lay the president's fundamental view of the crisis: Much as he wanted the Russians out of Cuba, he could not get past the thought that they had as much right to be there as the United States had in Turkey.

Turkey had been promised fifteen Jupiter medium-range missiles as a token of NATO support when the Soviets first deployed similar rockets on their own soil to threaten targets in Western Europe. The Jupiters could be fired only with the consent of both the American NATO commander and Turkish authorities. They stood near the Aegean coast, poised to strike the Soviet Union with warheads a hundred times more powerful than those dropped on Hiroshima. Like thirty other Jupiters in Italy, they were meant to sustain the morale of vulnerable allies. But it had taken until March 1962 to deploy and install them, by which time they were already obsolete.

In their own councils, American officials spoke of the Jupiters as burdensome duds that could be disabled by a single rifle shot. Eisenhower thought they should have been dumped at sea rather than promised to Turkey. His secretary of state, John Foster Dulles, thought it would be "quite wrong to assume that Europe wants these missiles." McNamara called them "a pile of junk." Rusk remembered how diplomats "joked about which way those missiles would go if they were fired." By mid-1962, they were wholly superfluous because missile-firing Polaris submarines were stationed in nearby waters and could reliably threaten many more Soviet targets.

But the Turks rebuffed all suggestions that they give up the Jupiters and trust in Polaris instead. They thought withdrawal of the missiles from their territory would look like a withdrawal of America's commitment to their defense. So Rusk and his ambassadors had not pressed the issue. Now, in a crisis, U.S. diplomats feared that any deal to swap the missiles in Turkey for those in Cuba would strike all European allies as a betrayal. As Bundy put it, the NATO nations would never understand why the United States refused to live, as they had long lived, within range of Soviet missiles. The Germans especially would conclude that America's jitters about a few rockets in Cuba would further jeopardize hard-to-defend Berlin.

WHEN THIS FIRST SEARCH for a strategy bogged down, Kennedy changed the subject. He wondered again about Khrushchev's motives and tried to see the world through his eyes. What was he really after? It must be, he guessed shrewdly, that the Soviets were not satisfied with their intercontinental missiles; General Taylor had often told him the Soviet ICBMs were seriously defective. As almost everyone in ExCom knew, the United States could deliver about five thousand warheads or bombs to Soviet targets, a seventeen-to-one margin over the three hundred nukes that could be carried by inferior Soviet missiles and planes. So since Khrushchev had no hope of gaining a great military advantage, he must be angling for political dividends.

Putting more American targets within range of Soviet MRBMs "makes them look like they're co-equal with us," the president observed in answer to his own question. The purpose must be to impress Latin America with support for Cuba, to enhance the Soviet Union's influence everywhere, and especially to invigorate its diplomacy in Europe. Rusk added the thought that the Soviets were inspired by the American bases in Turkey "to sort of balance that political, psychological flank," leading to the same conclusion: They could then "bargain Berlin and Cuba against each other" or "provoke us into a kind of action in Cuba which would give an umbrella for them to take action with respect to Berlin." He was beginning to wonder "whether maybe Mr. Khrushchev is entirely rational about Berlin."

Turkey. Berlin. The NATO alliance. The eyes of ExCom were fixed on a threat in Cuba, but in heart and mind the president and his closest aides were most concerned about the defense of Europe, the respect and cohesion of the Western allies, and, of course, their political vulnerability at home.

Perceiving no easy plan for action, Kennedy wondered how much time he could take to reach a decision. McNamara urged speed; if ordered to attack, he wanted to strike before the Soviet missiles in Cuba could fire back. The military chiefs wanted not only speed but also the advantage of surprise. But the diplomats preferred to give the Russians some kind of warning, buying time to negotiate. So the consensus was that the president had at most a week to decide, time that the Pentagon needed in any case to prepare for action.

The cacophony of counsel obviously haunted the president as he lunched with the crown prince of Libya and during the off-the-record remarks he delivered afterward to a meeting of several hundred editors and reporters at the State Department. I happened to be in his audience, which knew nothing about the storm building in the Caribbean. So most of us were startled to hear Kennedy's untypical pessimism. This handsome, vigorous, witty leader was suddenly doubting that the human race could safely reach the end of this nuclear century. I heard a British journalist behind me whisper that leaders were not supposed to talk that way; even in the darkest hours of

World War II, Winston Churchill would say, "Stick with me, I'll get you through this."

Just then, Kennedy reached into his pocket and read out a verse that he attributed to a Spanish torero:

> *Bullfight critics, row on row,*
> *Crowd the enormous plaza full.*
> *But only one is there who knows,*
> *And he's the one who fights the bull.*

IN A MEETING WITHOUT their matador, upstairs at the State Department, three strong voices were now raised in favor of negotiating before attacking. Adlai Stevenson, the articulate ambassador to the United Nations (and oft-defeated rival of the president), joined two old Soviet hands, Bohlen and Thompson, in arguing to Rusk that there was still time to make a deal with Khrushchev. At the Pentagon, however, the Joint Chiefs were hardening their demand for an all-out attack. They said they would rather do nothing than attempt a limited strike at only missile bases, as the president seemed to favor. They would promise success only if allowed to bomb all available targets throughout the island and, ideally, allowed to follow up with an invasion.

By Tuesday evening, when the ExCom reassembled at the White House, the debate was pretty well defined. Rusk and his fellow diplomats wanted to warn the Russians that they faced an attack if Khrushchev did not agree within twenty-four hours to withdraw the missiles from Cuba. A surprise attack, they warned, could arouse enough anger in Latin America to undermine the stability of several friendly governments. A surprise attack could also provoke a Soviet counteraction in Europe, which would surely split the Western alliance.

The trouble was that Ted Sorensen's backstage efforts to draft a warning letter to Khrushchev failed to satisfy the president. It was easy enough to compose a warning and a demand for withdrawal, but when it came to the "or else," the letters sounded unacceptably provocative. And any such notice, Kennedy realized, would shift the initiative for action back to Khrushchev.

McNamara had by now correctly read Kennedy's objections to both the diplomatic and military options, perhaps from conferring with Robert Kennedy. And he came prepared Tuesday evening to suggest a middle course. Diplomacy alone, he summarized, would yield no good result and cause an unacceptable delay. Military action risked a bloody conflict in Cuba and a Soviet counterblow elsewhere. He therefore favored a blockade around Cuba to stop all shipments of offensive weapons, combined with vigorous reconnaissance over the island and a warning to the Russians that any attack on the United States from Cuba would be treated as an attack by them. This plan might not sound attractive, McNamara concluded, "but wait until you work on the others."

He had obviously worked on them all. His proposal combined a modest military measure—the blockade—with a tough warning and demand that still left time to negotiate and to decide on further action. But his plan could not by itself compel removal of the missiles already unloaded in Cuba or stop construction at the missile sites.

Bundy, who justified his constant shifts of view as a duty to keep all options before the president, now wondered whether any action was really necessary. Yes, he said, the president had warned of "the gravest consequences" if missiles appeared in Cuba. But did the missiles gravely change the strategic balance?

"Not at all" was McNamara's instant opinion. But that was his personal view. He also replied for the Joint Chiefs, who thought the threat was "substantial." General Taylor, the chairman of the chiefs, tried to bridge the obvious gap in Pentagon assessments. From a cold-blooded point of view, he said, "these are just a few more missiles targeted on the United States." But once established, the Soviet bases

were sure to be improved and expanded indefinitely, greatly aug-
menting Soviet power.

The president agreed that the bases could keep on growing. The
idea of doing nothing was never raised again.

McNamara's blockade idea was gaining favor, but there was as yet
no limit on the kind of action the Kennedy brothers were willing to
examine. If the choice was to attack, the president still preferred a surgical strike at the missiles alone, but he told the chiefs to plan also for
a full-scale invasion. Robert Kennedy even strained to find a pretext
for invasion. He toyed with the thought of staging a fake attack on the
American naval base at Guantánamo or staging another ship disaster
in Havana—"sink the *Maine* again, or something." He remarked with
satisfaction that an invasion would get rid of Castro as well as the missiles.

These were attitudes brought over from a separate high-level
meeting that day in which Robert Kennedy had complained about the
slow pace of sabotage and subversion against Cuba under Operation
Mongoose. But his wild mood shifts were surely confusing to the conferees as they tried to discern the direction of the president's thinking.
Only that morning, at the first ExCom meeting, Bobby had scribbled
a note to Ted Sorensen saying, "I now know how Tojo felt when he
was planning Pearl Harbor." With Bobby's encouragement, historians were later led to read that note as a high-minded aversion to surprise attack. In context, however, it was more an ironic comment on
Robert's own belligerence at this stage.

POLITICAL CONSIDERATIONS WERE NOT much discussed in
ExCom, but they never left the president's consciousness. On
Wednesday, October 17—Day 2 of ExCom's deliberation—Kennedy
sent McCone to solicit President Eisenhower's support for whatever
he finally decided to do. And after keeping appointments with the

West German foreign minister and Libyan crown prince, the president actually left Washington to campaign for Connecticut's Abe Ribicoff, to whom he "owed one" for his early support in the 1960 presidential election.

In the president's absence, the ExCom meeting lost all focus. It featured an animated debate between thirty-seven-year-old Robert Kennedy and Dean Acheson, the crusty sixty-nine-year-old former secretary of state, whose judgment the president had invited. Acheson disdained the disorder in the room. He thought the Russians had been sufficiently warned to justify an air strike against the missile bases. He resented Robert Kennedy's claim that a surprise attack would amount to "another Pearl Harbor" and quickly withdrew from the deliberation.

FIDEL CASTRO, IN ANY CASE, did not intend to be surprised. He did not know that the missile sites had been discovered. But the U.S. naval maneuvers in the Caribbean were alarming enough to cause him to order a "maximum alert" of his army and militia. According to one former aide, Castro also prepared two forms of retaliation in case Americans invaded his island. One plan envisioned covert attacks on U.S. personnel and facilities in Latin America. The other, called "Operation Boomerang," called for Cubans stationed at the United Nations to organize acts of terror around New York City.[10]

ON HIS RETURN TO THE CAPITAL Wednesday evening President Kennedy found a flurry of individual memos that pointed to the same

---

[10] These plans were reported by Domingo Amuchastegui, a former political officer for Cuba's General Staff and intelligence officer in the armed forces, as cited in *Intelligence and the Cuban Missile Crisis*, James G. Blight and David A. Welch, editors. Portland, OR: Frank Cass, 1988.

division he had heard the night before. Bohlen and Thompson, speaking as Kremlinologists, cautioned against thinking only about Cuba; they thought Berlin was Khrushchev's true objective and therefore felt he had to be confronted directly. Like McNamara, they urged combining a demand for withdrawal of the missiles with a blockade to prevent further shipments.

The military chiefs continued to argue for at least five hundred air sorties. McCone, a pivotal figure because of his Republicanism and accurate predictions about Soviet intentions, favored an ultimatum that warned of massive air strikes unless the missiles were removed within twenty-four hours. Adlai Stevenson proposed a deal to dismantle Soviet and American missile bases all across the globe. Rusk's deputy, George Ball, and Douglas Dillon, a Republican serving as secretary of the treasury, endorsed a blockade, thinking it might even bring down Castro. Sorensen refined McNamara's list of options in such a way that a blockade combined with a warning of further action looked to be the moderate middle course.

The Kennedy brothers and Sorensen functioned as a kind of ExCom within ExCom, consulting with advisers of their choice out of range of the hidden microphones. Their private calculations were not recorded, therefore, but Sorensen left many lists that he composed to try to clarify the president's choices. He also drafted speeches and letters to Khrushchev that tested the language and logic the president might use with various strategies. In this troika's view late Wednesday, a naval blockade of some kind looked to be the best idea. But at that very moment, the photo analysts across town detected new activity on the films from Cuba, activity that significantly altered the ExCom's perception of the Soviet threat.

PORING OVER MILES OF NEW U-2 film, the analysts observed rapid progress at the previously detected sites of mobile launchers for

MRBMs—at San Cristóbal, 50 miles southwest of Havana, and 130 miles east in central Cuba, at Sagua la Grande. But they also found unmistakable evidence of the building of fixed launch sites for intermediate-range missiles—one set near Guanajay, 25 miles southwest of Havana, and one 170 miles to the east, near Remedios. When completed, these IRBMs would be able to strike at targets almost anywhere in the continental United States, to a range of twenty-two hundred miles.

That news changed everything, Rusk declared at the start of Thursday's meeting. Cuba was no longer "just an incidental base for a few of these things." It could become "a formidable military problem in any contest we would have with the Soviet Union." American "inaction" would undermine the nation's alliances and encourage Soviet adventures elsewhere. But the now alarmed secretary of state still worried that attacking the Soviet bases ran the risk of igniting a wider war. Having witnessed the public's weariness with war in Korea when he had charge of Far East policy, Rusk cautioned that whatever was done had better be clearly explained and justified to the American people. And the diplomat in him said Khrushchev ought to be given the chance, no matter how slight, to back down before the shooting started. The missiles had changed, but the available choices had not.

McNamara, too, stiffened the sound of his voice, but it still trembled with ambiguity. He said the new information moved him toward the view of the Joint Chiefs, who wanted to attack most military targets in Cuba in a single day. They would not destroy every last missile, but quick action would surely prevent any counterattack against the United States. Yet McNamara still doubted that the Soviet bases posed much of a military danger. "It's a political problem," he said. "It's a problem of holding the alliance together. It's a problem of properly conditioning Khrushchev for our future moves." These concerns and "the problem of dealing with our domestic public" all pointed toward action that the military threat itself might not require.

Kennedy became the last skeptic standing. He looked at himself and his choices through European and Latin eyes. Would friendly nations really applaud his attacking Cuba? Mindful of the Bay of Pigs fiasco, did not the allies already think "that we're slightly demented on this subject" of Cuba? No matter how disturbing the new photos, "a lot of people would regard this as a mad act by the United States," especially if the secretary of defense, looking at the problem with American eyes, did not really believe the military balance significantly threatened or altered.

So the president held out for a plan that would give Khrushchev "a chance to pull them out." And more: He wanted to sweeten the offer by telling Khrushchev that "if you begin to pull them out, we'll take ours out of Turkey." The only problem with this approach, he still worried, was that Khrushchev might refuse and then threaten to answer an attack on Cuba with an attack in Berlin.

Tommy Thompson, who never spent a Sunday in Moscow without hosting a high-bluff, low-stake game of poker ("the Kopek-Cabana," reporters called his table), now saw his chance to focus the discussion. He spoke up more firmly than anyone, encouraging what he recognized to be the president's deepest instincts.

"My preference is this blockade plan," he said. "I think it's very highly doubtful that the Russians would resist a blockade against military weapons, particularly offensive ones, if that's the way we pitched it before the world."

Through the babble of other comments around the large table, the president and former ambassador now pursued the most acute conversation of the entire week.

"What do we do with the weapons already there?" Kennedy asked.

"Demand they're dismantled and say that we're going to maintain constant surveillance and if they are armed, we would then take them out—and then maybe do it," Thompson replied. This approach might still result in a military strike, he conceded, "but we do it in an entirely different posture and background and much less danger of getting up into the big war." Moreover, he added, the Russians have "a curious faculty of wanting a legal basis, despite all of the outrageous things they've done." They would not lightly challenge a blockade that had been legally established, maybe with a declaration of war.

"As Chip [Bohlen] says," Thompson added, "I agree with him, that if they're prepared to say: 'All right, if you do this then this is nuclear world war,' then they would do that anyway. I think [Khrushchev] would make a lot of threatening language but in very vague terms in keeping his—"

"Yeah," Kennedy interjected. "I would think it more like he would just grab Berlin."

"I think that," Thompson said, "or, if we just made the first strike, then I think his answer would be, very probably, to take out one of our bases in Turkey and make it quick, too, and then say that, 'Now I want to talk.' I think the whole purpose of this exercise is to build up to talks with you, in which we try to negotiate out the bases. There are a lot of things that point to that. One thing that struck me very much is, if it's so easy to camouflage these things or to hide them in the woods, why didn't they do it in the first place? They surely expected us to see them at some stage. That, it seems, would point to the fact their purpose was for preparation of negotiations." That the Soviets wanted the deployment to be discovered was one of Thompson's few false assumptions, but it led him nonetheless to a correct conclusion about negotiation.

Other voices predicted that the Soviet answer to a blockade of Cuba would be a blockade of Berlin, at the least. And Robert Kennedy cautioned that a blockade of Cuba would be "a very slow death"—the crisis would drag on for months with all sides screaming threats and Russian ships being confronted and maybe planes being shot down.

Thompson's answer to all these doubts was that Khrushchev would say, " 'What are you getting so excited about? The Cubans asked us for some missiles to deal with these [Cuban] émigré bases that . . . are threatening to attack. . . . These are not missiles other than defensive. They're much less offensive than your weapons in Turkey. . . . We haven't given any nuclear weapons to [the Cubans]. These are simply to deal with the threat to Cuba.' "

And here Thompson reached the nub of his counsel: "You want to make it—if you do any of these steps—make it as easy as possible for him to back down."

McCone's reaction was to warn that negotiation would tie America's hands indefinitely, an objection that the president answered by invoking his fallback sweetener: The only way of "giving him some out, would be our Turkey missiles." Bundy suggested bombing Cuba and offering up the Turkey bases simultaneously. But Rusk warned that a Cuba–Turkey swap would undermine the NATO alliance. McNamara predicted that the price of a deal—removing American missiles from Turkey and Italy—was likely to be the same with or without military action; therefore talking before the shooting started had the advantage of not killing several hundred Russians. (At this stage, the ExCom thought there were five to ten thousand Soviet troops on the island when in fact there were more than forty-two thousand!)

Still looking at himself through foreign eyes, Kennedy speculated that if Khrushchev were to grab Berlin, the allies would feel America had lost that treasured outpost because of its stubborn refusal to tolerate missiles that Western Europe had lived with for quite some time.

"My guess," Thompson interjected, "is that he would not immediately attack Berlin, but he would precipitate the real crisis at first in order to try to sap our morale."

But wasn't Khrushchev planning to grab Berlin *after* he unveiled the Cuban missiles in November? And wouldn't any effort to defend Berlin with nuclear artillery shatter the Western alliance? Kennedy succinctly summarized his dilemma: A wider conflict resulting from an attack on Cuba would undermine the alliance, but so would his failure to stand up to the Russians. So he clung to the blockade idea, wondering now whether he would really have to declare war on Cuba just to make a blockade appear legal in Soviet eyes.

No, he was told, it could be made to appear legal by a vote of hemisphere nations invoking the Rio Treaty of joint defense— provided the ever sensitive governments of Latin America could be persuaded for once to support the United States against a small neighbor.

McCone still doubted that Khrushchev would respect a blockade, but Thompson elaborated on his analysis: "I don't think he'd want to take military action around Cuba. He's too much at a disadvantage there. It would be more dangerous than somewhere else. That's why I think he might respect [a blockade] or maybe he takes the big action in Berlin—which is this gamble which he's shown, *for four years*, he's reluctant to take."

Despite some resistance around the table, the advocates of negoti- ation lined up behind Thompson as he offered yet another benefit: Khrushchev would have to discuss the president's challenge with col- leagues in the Kremlin, "and there is a possibility of restraint there." He recalled how Soviet military leaders at the Paris summit of 1960 had openly revealed to Americans their belief "that Khrushchev was being impetuous and running risks."

So the benefit of notifying Khrushchev was that he might back down? Kennedy asked.

The first advantage, Thompson answered, was that "if we eventu- ally face the crunch on Berlin" some allies would still support the United States out of respect for its restraint. Second, yes, was the chance that Khrushchev would back down. And third was the oppor- tunity to get into negotiation with him.

Tipping his hand some more, Kennedy asked about the best way to communicate with Khrushchev. But he kept prodding the Penta- gon to be ready to back up diplomacy with credible threats of military action. He was told an air attack could occur as soon as Monday, four days hence, and an invasion of Cuba could start a week or ten days later.

Although he was close to a decision, Kennedy was persuaded not even to hint at the missile discovery when the Soviet foreign minister, Andrei Gromyko, came calling at the White House Thursday afternoon. Though scheduled in calmer times, the encounter became a dramatic highlight of the crisis.

IT WAS TOMMY THOMPSON's picaresque analogy that persuaded the president to hide his fury as Gromyko perpetuated the Soviet missile deception. It's rather like a wife finding out you've been unfaithful, Thompson said without irony to his philandering president. "She may know, but when you tell her, things . . . will begin to happen."

So the aerial photos stayed hidden in his Oval Office desk while Kennedy rocked in his chair and baited Gromyko to come clean. Without mentioning missiles, the president said that Soviet arms shipments to Cuba had produced "the most dangerous situation" since World War II. He even reread his September warnings about "grave" consequences. But the Soviet foreign minister proved Khrushchev's judgment of him—that he could, if ordered, sit naked on a block of ice. He kept emphasizing Khrushchev's desire to wait until after the November elections to deal with Berlin, calling it a "rotten tooth which must be pulled out." As for Cuba, he lied, the Russians were only training Cubans in the use of "defensive weapons" to guard against invasion. "If it were otherwise," Gromyko said, mimicking the very words the president had used to warn of grave consequences, the Soviet government would have never become involved in Cuba.

Well, as a matter of fact, the president countered, there never was any danger of invasion. He had no intention of invading Cuba. And he would have readily given Khrushchev that assurance if only he'd been asked.

At that moment, this presidential comment was merely pointing to a missed opportunity. No one yet realized that Kennedy had, unwittingly, pointed a path out of the crisis.

KENNEDY ALSO MET THAT DAY with Acheson, an admired, tough diplomat, to let him vent against brother Bobby's "high school thought" that an air attack would amount to "a Pearl Harbor in reverse." The insult must have reminded Kennedy of how Acheson, after the Bay of Pigs, had called the president "a gifted amateur practicing with a boomerang and suddenly knocking himself cold." But Kennedy let the slur against Bobby glide by. He understood Acheson's advice, and planned to ignore it.

"I guess I better earn my salary this week," the president remarked.

"I'm afraid you have to," Acheson replied. "I wish I could be more help." He was astutely sure that the president had made up his mind.

That he had. But Kennedy's quest for political cover continued. He turned next to Robert Lovett, the equally respected former secretary of defense and prominent member of the "Eastern Establishment" of Republican lawyers and financiers. Duly briefed on his way into the Oval Office, Lovett quickly endorsed a blockade "as the first step" because, he said, he agreed with Robert Kennedy that "we could always blow the place up if necessary."

Thursday evening, Rusk and Thompson entertained Gromyko at a State Department dinner while one floor below the rest of ExCom continued to plot its surprise against the Soviets. It was there that Leonard Meeker, the department's deputy legal adviser, first proposed calling the blockade a "quarantine." Although mainly a propaganda ploy, this semantic switch served to remind the group that its second move also did not have to be a military attack. If the "quarantine" against offensive weapons proved inadequate, it could be broadened to bar not only offensive weapons but also oil and other military essentials. In yet a further step, it could become a total blockade against all shipping so as to gradually strangle the Cuban economy.

The prospect of gradual escalation to propel the negotiations with Khrushchev obviously appealed to the president. He called the ExCom back to the White House after 9 PM Thursday to order planning for a limited blockade, to be publicly called a quarantine. The conferees were so afraid that a late-night parade of limousines would betray their crisis conference that nine of them piled into a single sedan, drove to the Treasury, and trooped through an underground tunnel to the family quarters of the White House. Around midnight, the president went alone to the Oval Office and spoke his personal conclusions into a tape recorder, a report to history.

"The consensus was that we should go ahead with the blockade," he dictated, and "that we could tighten the blockade as the situation requires. I was most anxious that we not have to announce a state of war existing, because it would obviously be bad to have the word go out that we were having a war rather than that it was a limited blockade for a limited purpose."

PRUDENCE WAS THE WATCHWORD also in Cuba that night among the Soviet members of General Gribkov's inspection party. He had flown from Moscow to deliver Defense Minister Malinovsky's stern reminder to the local commander, General Pliyev, that nuclear weapons—the MRBMs, IRBMs, coastal cruise missiles, and Luna artillery weapons—were to be fired only with Khrushchev's personal permission.

"We do not intend to unleash an atomic war; that is not in our interests," he remembered saying. The orders at this stage foresaw only one exception to the no-nukes rule: "In an extreme situation," if there was no way to communicate with Moscow and American troops were actually landing in Cuba, then the Luna nuclear artillery weapons might be used—though not "in haste."

Pliyev, the local commander, struck Gribkov as ill from heat and humidity and discouraged by construction delays. The MRBM bases were not going to be finished on schedule by October 26–27. Rocky topsoil was resisting Soviet machinery, and security made it impossible to use Cuban labor. The hot sun left Russian tents and trailers almost uninhabitable, even at night, and mosquitoes made the open air equally intolerable. Worse still, Pliyev thought the missiles had probably been discovered by American U-2s. The spy planes were flying many missions across Cuba and with impunity, because the Soviet antiaircraft missiles, though fully installed, had orders to defend only against attack, not against reconnaissance.

The general's fear of discovery, however, was not conveyed to the Kremlin. In fact, Gromyko left Washington on Friday after smugly informing Khrushchev that the Cuban situation was "wholly satisfactory." His cable to Moscow failed to find any significance in the fact that "Rusk sat silently and was as red as a lobster" during his White House joust with Kennedy. Gromyko felt sure that the United States "has put its money on obstructing Cuba's economic relations . . . to cause hunger in the country . . . and prompting an uprising against the regime." At his obsequious best, Gromyko concluded that American "ruling circles are amazed by the Soviet Union's courage in assisting Cuba . . . [and] in these conditions a USA military adventure against Cuba is almost impossible to imagine."

As Ambassador Dobrynin observed in his memoir, "Never before had the experienced and cautious Gromyko made so grave a miscalculation!"

. . .

KENNEDY HAD OUTPERFORMED Gromyko but he faced still greater tests of his acting skills on Friday, when he finally confronted the Joint Chiefs of Staff before flying off on what was advertised as a three-day campaign tour of seven states.

The president knew the chiefs wanted a massive surprise attack on Cuba, advice that he had rejected. He would not have it said, however, that he never heard their arguments firsthand. With McNamara and Taylor at his side, Kennedy engaged the individual chiefs—General Curtis LeMay, the pugnacious leader of the air force, still highly respected for his World War II derring-do and commander of the airlift that had broken the Berlin blockade; General Earle Wheeler of the army, an accomplished planner and Pentagon politician; Admiral George Anderson, known throughout the navy as a "straight arrow"; and General David Shoup of the marines, a tough, crude, highly decorated combat veteran.

The president preempted the opening minutes of the meeting to explain his preference—and obvious decision—for a blockade and his hope that it would compel a negotiated and favorable outcome. The chiefs referred contemptuously to this approach as mere "political action" and "talk." The president tried hard to hide his mistrust of the bemedaled men before him, the same chiefs who had failed him by not critiquing the CIA's invasion plan for the Bay of Pigs and failed again recently by not providing a swift show of force to preserve order at the University of Mississippi. Kennedy also muffled what he knew would irritate the military mind: his intention to use the forces arrayed in the Caribbean not to wage war but to send a diplomatic message to Moscow. Only hours earlier, he had remarked to O'Donnell that "these brass hats have one great advantage in their favor. If we listen to them, and do what they want us to do, none of us will be alive later to tell them that they were wrong."

Still, Kennedy recited his reasoning respectfully. If he did nothing, he told the chiefs, the Russians would have gained an important base in Cuba and damaged American prestige the world over. But if he attacked without warning, as they wanted, he would provoke—and justify—Soviet action in Berlin. And that might force him to resort to nuclear weapons, inviting the contempt of the allies for "trigger-happy Americans."

The chiefs would have none of it. General LeMay doubted the Russians would retaliate for an attack in Cuba. A blockade, he warned dismissively, would only drive their mobile missiles into the woods. And "political action"—negotiation—would only lead to war. His defiant conclusion was that the president's chosen course "is almost as bad as the appeasement [of Hitler] at Munich." Admiral Anderson concurred: Only a surprise attack would prevent the missiles being fired against the United States; a blockade was sure to intensify the threat. General Wheeler argued that the Russians' deployment stood to gain them a "quantum jump" in ability to damage the United States. The army chief thought foreigners and Americans alike would look upon a blockade and political talk as "a pretty weak response."

"In other words," LeMay concluded, "you're in a pretty bad fix at the present time."

"What did you say?" a startled president asked.

"You're in a pretty bad fix."

With a forced laugh, Kennedy answered, "You're in there with me—personally."

When the president left the meeting to begin his campaign trip, General Shoup let loose with angry expletives. He boasted that they had finally "forced" the president to acknowledge that instead of decisive action he wanted to practice feeble "escalation."

"If only somebody could keep them from doing the goddamn thing piecemeal," Shoup said bitterly. "That's our problem. You go in there and friggin' around with the missiles. You're screwed." LeMay agreed.

Heading for his plane, the president was further irritated by Bundy's third change of heart in three days. Having begun the week in favor of an air strike, then switched to supporting a blockade, then shifted again to favor doing nothing until the Soviets actually threatened Berlin, Bundy had decided overnight to rejoin the air attack faction. Kennedy wearily indulged him, telling him to keep all options open. But that was playacting as well. He simultaneously told his brother and Sorensen to pull the ExCom to a consensus during his absence—a consensus of support, of course, for what he intended to do.

And if they failed?

"I'll make my own decision anyway."

SEVEN

ONLY ONE WILL
FACE THE BULL

HARD AS IT WAS, DECIDING WHAT TO DO PROVED TO BE the easy part of Kennedy's crisis performance. Jousting with Khrushchev in an exchange of messages was as tough as trading blows on a battlefield.

By choosing a strategy that hovered halfway between mere negotiation and direct military action, the president had actually deferred the tough decisions. He was still free to decide whether to attack, and when, and with how much force, and whether and when to offer concessions. By combining a "quarantine" with the threat of further action, he had also won over two important Republicans in ExCom, McCone and Dillon, and preserved a broad consensus to withstand the opposition of the Joint Chiefs and their friends in Congress. But the president had not really committed himself to any further action. Even the blockade remained to be defined; he could stop all Cuba-bound Soviet ships, or some, or none. He could negotiate for weeks, or days, or hours before shooting at a disobedient ship's propeller, bombing a missile base, or sending his armies to conquer Cuba. The president did resolve to attack any antiaircraft battery that shot down a U-2 spy plane; reconnaissance was crucial to measure Soviet intentions. But he kept control of every military move, every diplomatic proposal, and every public statement.

Since the Russians could not yet be told about the discovery of the missiles, neither could the American people. And so the U.S. government's dissembling became chronic. The Pentagon simply lied when reporters asked about missiles in Cuba, and it later defended its right to lie in such circumstances. More subtly, the State Department maintained that Secretary Rusk had canceled a Friday night speech because of "the press of routine business." The Joint Chiefs of Staff canceled all their speeches for what they alleged was work "on the budget." Our intimations of crisis at *The Times* were confirmed when midlevel officials fled their own dinner parties, one his own birthday celebration. Spotting all these schedule changes, reporters in Washington recognized the scent of a big story. Bundy tried to mislead us by mentioning trouble over Berlin, but when I called the West German ambassador at his home at 10:30 PM Friday, he'd gone to bed. "Can't possibly be Berlin," I told my colleagues even before the ambassador came to the phone and sleepily said he knew of nothing unusual back home.

The president sent word through aides to our bureau chief, Scotty Reston, that he knew we would soon figure out what had happened and he asked to be called before *The Times* printed anything. That spurred our search for the source of the trouble, and it took only another twenty-four hours to eliminate Southeast Asia. So the trouble lay in Latin America, and the summerlong semantic squabble with Republicans about "offensive" versus "defensive" weapons in Cuba made it fairly easy to deduce the discovery of offensive missiles.

In yet another act of pretense, Kennedy flew to Chicago on Friday, October 19, to endorse the Senate candidacy of Sidney Yates—when in fact he hoped, at the urging of Vice President Lyndon Johnson, for the reelection of Yates's opponent, Senator Everett Dirksen, the malleable leader of the Republican minority. Then, Saturday morning, instead of flying on to scheduled rallies in St. Louis, Albuquerque, and Seattle, Kennedy summoned Rear Admiral George Burkley, the White House physician, and ordered him to diagnose a presidential cold. Kennedy handed Pierre Salinger a note for announcement to the traveling White House press corps: "Slight upper respiratory; one degree temp; weather raw and rainy; recommended return to Washington, cancel schedule."

As Kennedy carried his theatrics onto Air Force One, he defied habit by wearing a felt hat. Salinger now demanded to know what strange things were happening. He would find out in Washington, the president replied, "And when you do, grab your balls."

The presidential "cold" was catching. When Vice President Johnson, too, cut short a campaign trip in Hawaii, reporters kidded Salinger about the governmental epidemic. We took the spreading sniffles as confirmation that momentous events were at hand.

The clues that pointed to Cuba could no longer be denied. What we never learned was the extent of Kennedy's real illness and how much pain he endured daily from assorted ailments and medications. We always suspected from his red cheeks that he was taking cortisone, for acknowledged back spasms, but we knew nothing of the mad combination of drugs that was revealed only decades later to be swirling in his system. Yet the verbatim record of his conduct in these tense days yields no hint of intellectual dysfunction.

Kennedy returned to Washington after lunch Saturday, October 20, and took a pain-relieving swim while Bobby briefed him on developments from the edge of the White House pool. Sorensen had drafted a speech to be delivered on television Monday evening. The latest U-2 intelligence showed that sixteen of at least twenty-four MRBM launchers appeared to be operational, while eight IRBM launchers (of an eventual sixteen) looked to be a month or six weeks from completion. The analysts had not spotted any nuclear warheads but assumed they were destined to be stored in what looked like bunkers a few miles from Havana. The intelligence teams were still

underestimating the number of Soviet troops on the island. And not
for decades would Americans be told that those Soviet troops possessed a dozen nuclear artillery shells for possible use against an invasion force. In a dismaying but possibly coordinated development,
Communist China and India that day allowed their border disputes to
break out into open warfare.

In his only display of nervousness, Kennedy phoned his wife,
Jacqueline, on Saturday afternoon, and asked her to return with their
two children from a Virginia horse farm so that the family could be
together in the coming days.

The president let the ExCom vent some more but held doggedly
to his plan. He would order a "quarantine" of Cuba to prevent its further import of "offensive" weapons and equipment, and he would
threaten further action if the missiles on the island were not withdrawn. His choice of a limited blockade, however, still invited debate
about the language he should use to define his tactics.

Adlai Stevenson wanted the blockade to be combined with an
overt bid to negotiate; he suggested offering the withdrawal of Jupiter
missiles from Europe and the navy's withdrawal from Guantánamo.
The Republicans in ExCom angrily denounced that idea; they wanted
an air strike if the Soviets failed to stop work on the Cuban bases. Mc-
Namara also favored negotiation during the blockade and suggested
the bait of an eventual rather than immediate withdrawal from Guantánamo. Kennedy rejected bargaining with the naval base as a sign of
weakness. But he said again that a deal for the Jupiters in Turkey and
Italy would probably be necessary. He refused to propose such a swap
of bases at the outset because that would suggest "we were in a state
of panic." He did, however, want the Turks and Italians to be told at
once that the Jupiters would not be fired under any circumstances,
even if attacked. And he called for a quick study of the consequences
of closing down the Jupiter bases.

As for military action, the president wanted the Pentagon to prepare for a quick strike as soon as Tuesday, but only against missile

sites. He still refused to fix either a time or circumstance for such an attack. As for invasion, he wanted it clearly understood that "no orders for that have been given; I've only said we'd be prepared."

The president's decisions were most warmly endorsed by his brother and by Thompson, Dillon, and McCone. Later on Saturday night, Kennedy went out of his way to telephone McCone to assure him that his advice had prevailed. He wanted the man who had guessed right about Soviet intentions—and who stood closest to Eisenhower—to feel fully vindicated and satisfied.

General Taylor, however, returned to the Pentagon Saturday night to tell the chiefs that "this was not one of our better days." He said the president knew they were unhappy but expected them to support his strategy. General Wheeler, the army chief of staff, shuddered with disappointment, saying, "I never thought I'd live to see the day when I would want to go to war."

ON SUNDAY, OCTOBER 21, all efforts shifted to planning for military contingencies, to designing the ultimatum that the president would give the Russians on Monday, and to the pursuit of international support.

The Pentagon refined its long-standing plans for attacking Cuba, but delayed more troop and air movements until the crisis could be openly acknowledged. It reckoned that an invasion could begin one week after five hundred air sorties had destroyed most Soviet planes in Cuba and perhaps 90 percent of the known missiles. A force of twenty-five thousand men would be put ashore in the first wave, and a total of ninety thousand within two weeks.

Admiral Anderson reported that forty ships stood by to enforce the blockade. He hoped the Russians could be given one day's warning, to let them send new instructions to the thirty Cuba-bound cargo vessels the navy had tracked at sea. He planned to follow established international rules for stopping and boarding vessels, disabling and

towing disobedient ones to an American port. He thought any submarine that tried to run the blockade should be destroyed.

The State Department asked Latin nations to give the quarantine
a legal cover by condemning the Soviet bases as a threat to the hemisphere and invoking the mutual defense provisions of the OAS treaty.
This was to be the legal sanction for blockade with which Tommy
Thompson wanted to impress the Soviet leaders.

In a remarkable display of diplomatic orchestration, the State Department also produced fifteen presidential letters and messages of
explanation to more than four hundred recipients around the globe,
with instructions for their delivery at designated times. It prepared
oral briefings for ninety-five ambassadors in Washington; drafted
special texts for delivery to the United Nations and the Organization
of American States; and sent out warnings of hostile demonstrations
to 134 embassies and consulates. The major allies in London, Paris,
and Bonn were to be shown photos of the missile sites by special presidential emissaries.[11]

Kennedy himself gave the first foreign briefing to his close friend
David Ormsby-Gore, whom the British had shrewdly made their
ambassador in Washington. Trying again to look at the world
through Khrushchev's eyes, the president acknowledged a grudging
admiration for the Soviet challenge: If the United States reacted vi-
olently, then the Russians would gain a pretext for attacking Berlin;
if the United States accepted the missiles in Cuba, it would lose
stature among allies, particularly in Latin America. In a surge of self-
pity, the president lamented the failure to remove obsolete Jupiters
from Europe. He also complained about West Germany's refusal to
recognize the communist regime of East Germany, which would

---

[11] When Acheson, doing his duty despite his dissent, went to brief President
Charles de Gaulle of France, the general airily waved off the pictures, saying that
a great nation would not act forcefully if there were any doubt about the evidence. Moments later, with fascination, he closely studied the photos.

have greatly diminished his vulnerability in Berlin. Kennedy was grateful for his British friend's support of the blockade and arranged to provide regular reports to Prime Minister Macmillan, no doubt looking upon the British as a leaky supplementary channel for signaling Moscow.

Sitting down Sunday to edit the Kennedy television address, the ExCom members further refined the threats and commitments implicit in his chosen course. The president wanted to emphasize that the evidence of offensive missiles in Cuba had not reached him until the previous Tuesday—long *after* Republican senators had claimed to have news of them. Aware that there was nothing illegal about the Soviet missile deployment, the president wanted his speech to focus on Khrushchev's duplicity and to list his specific falsehoods. He did not want to reveal America's intelligence skills by citing the number of known missiles or missile sites. At Thompson's urging, the president directed the ultimatum at Khrushchev personally, to cross swords with the Soviet Union, not Cuba. No message would be sent to Castro, but the speech would include some special words of sympathy for the Cuban people.

In further editing, Kennedy removed Sorensen's graphic depiction of the horror of war. He deleted the accurate but brutally frank challenge that Khrushchev had to choose between fighting the American navy in American waters and abandoning his obligations to Castro. He removed an offer to meet with Khrushchev; he intended to hang tough until the Soviet leader revealed his own next move. In fact, Kennedy's speech suggested that it might take "months" of tense diplomacy to disable the missiles, and he eliminated the demand that they be taken out "forthwith." But the president rejected Rusk's proposal to invite United Nations inspectors to watch over the missile sites; Kennedy said he preferred to alarm the world's diplomats to spur them to propose ways out of the crisis.

Having plotted at least a dozen chess moves ahead, the president

assumed that Khrushchev, too, had prepared his responses in case
Washington caught him out in mid-deployment. Kennedy figured
that the Russians would respond to his challenge by speeding up work
at the bases, threatening to fire the missiles if Cuba were attacked, and
making some kind of move to begin squeezing the Western allies in
Berlin.

THE PRESIDENT STILL WANTED to take Khrushchev by surprise,
to assert his demands before the Soviet leader could utter any preemptive threat. And that now required persuading *The New York
Times* and *The Washington Post* to refrain from printing what they
were learning and deducing about the crisis. Once reporters had narrowed the problem to Cuba, they were sure that Republican senators
had correctly defined the Soviet buildup.

The publisher of the *Post*, Philip Graham, was a Kennedy booster
and easily persuaded. *The Times* was a slightly harder sell, mainly because it had come to regret its decision in 1961 to play down some as-
pects of a story heralding the Bay of Pigs invasion. Still, as promised,
Scotty Reston telephoned Kennedy to reveal that we were ready to
report the presence of Soviet missiles in Cuba.

And do you know what I'm going to do about it?[12]

*No, sir, we don't, except we know you promised to act and we hear you've
asked for television time tomorrow night.*

*That's right. I'm going to order a blockade—a blockade of all Soviet mis-
sile shipments to Cuba. If you reveal my plan, or print that we discovered
their missiles in Cuba, Khrushchev could beat us to the draw. He could make
some preemptive move or counter with an ultimatum that would force us to
take more violent action.*

---

[12] I overheard this conversation on an extension phone, but since it is reconstructed
from notes and memory, the words appear in italics rather than quotation marks.

You're asking us to suppress the news?

I'm asking you not to disclose what we've discovered in Cuba until I have a chance to deploy our ships and address the country and the Russians tomorrow night.

Well, Reston said, *that sounds like a reasonable request, but we down here only report the news. This is a decision the publisher will have to make. I'll pass on your request immediately.*

Give Orvil [Dryfoos] my regards and tell him to call me if he disagrees.

Some of us urged Reston to resist. We could not betray the president's off-the-record revelation about a blockade, but we alone, and presumably our competitors, had deduced the nature of the threat. A blockade (even if publicly called a "quarantine") was an act of war, and we would be letting the president go to war against the Soviet Union without any notice to either Congress or the public. Couldn't we at least tell our readers the nature of the crisis?

Our desire for a great story clearly outweighed our sense of duty to the White House, but we argued in the name of the public interest. Reston agreed and called the White House again to cross-examine the president.

Mr. President, one more question, if you will: We all remember the Bay of Pigs and our belief that more advance publicity might have spared the country that humiliation and spared our Cuban friends many casualties. If we hold out on our readers now, are we going to be in a war against the Russians before we print another edition? Some of us wonder whether you are asking for secrecy until after the shooting has begun.

Scotty, we've taken a whole week to plan our response. I'm going to order a blockade, it's the least I can do. But we will not immediately attack. You have my word of honor: There will be no bloodshed before I explain this very serious situation to the American people.

A presidential "word of honor" still carried weight in those years. Like *The Post,* we pulled our punch on Monday morning. The story I wrote described an "air of crisis" in the capital, hinted that Cuba was

involved, and predicted a Kennedy speech that evening. But it did not
mention missiles or blockade—or carry the byline of the article's
slightly embarrassed writer.

KENNEDY, LIKE KHRUSHCHEV, understood intuitively that policy
and publicity were inseparable twins, especially in crisis. But whereas
the Soviet leader spoke with a single, domineering voice, the president had to keep dozens of officials and politicians "on message." Any
number of them might, by design or inadvertence, misrepresent his
intentions, plans, and moods. The cacophony of a democracy can be
healthy or unsettling, but in a military confrontation it can become
downright dangerous. Managing the message, to friends and foes, was
Monday's main business.

In the president's view, Adlai Stevenson had shown himself too
eager to plunge into negotiations. To "stiffen" his spine at the United
Nations, Kennedy sent a military plane to Europe to bring back John
McCloy, a New York banker and unofficial "chairman" of the Eastern
Establishment of Republican public servants, who was persuaded to
serve as Stevenson's diplomatic chaperone.

Next came a call to former President Eisenhower to secure his
support even if things went awry. Kennedy gave him a gloomy forecast: He did *not* expect the Russians to withdraw or cease work on the
missiles. So he feared his U-2 spy planes would be shot down, forcing
an American air attack and Soviet retaliation in Berlin. Eisenhower
refused to join in the pessimism. He doubted that the Soviets would
connect Cuba to Berlin; he knew them to be much more improvisa-
tional, habitually engaged in ad hoc maneuvers, doing "just what they
find out they can do here and there and the other place."

But what if Khrushchev announced tomorrow that an attack on
Cuba would result in nuclear war, Kennedy asked; "what's your judgment as to the chances they'll fire these things off?"

"I don't believe that they will," Eisenhower replied soothingly. But "of course" the president needed to keep everyone very alert.

Kennedy chuckled. "Yeah. Well, we'll hang on tight."

Eisenhower, also chuckling, "Yes, sir."

After less tense calls to former presidents Hoover and Truman, Kennedy joined his brother and Rusk to edit Stevenson's presentation of the missile complaint to the United Nations. They decided for the time being not to release corroborating photographs but to let American journalists look at them. They called a special, larger ExCom meeting for later Monday to rehearse "all the dirty questions" they would face. Then, trying to anticipate the effects of the crisis in Europe, Kennedy said he could not trust the Joint Chiefs to have firmly guarded against a panicky firing of the Jupiter missiles; he wanted new, clear instructions sent directly to the missile units. Bundy mockingly saluted his "doubting master."

At noon Monday, October 22, still seven hours before the toss of the gauntlet, the ExCom was suddenly thrown off stride by news that Foreign Minister Gromyko planned "a major announcement" in New York. Afraid that Khrushchev was about to acknowledge "defensive" missiles in Cuba and warn against American action, Kennedy rushed preparations for his own crisis declaration. But two hours later, the Soviet announcement turned out to be a routine farewell statement from Gromyko as he flew off to Moscow from New York. It was only the first misfired communication in a fateful week of crossed wires.

When the ExCom gathered to prepare for "dirty questions," Kennedy wanted his spokesmen to stress three reasons for the risks he was running: first, he felt obligated to honor his public commitment to resist the shipment of "offensive" weapons to Cuba; second, the secret Soviet deployment was such a departure from past policy that a failure to respond would cause the Russians to conclude "that we would never act, no matter what they did anywhere"; and third, any

Soviet action against West Berlin would find them doing in October what they planned in any case for November, not something provoked by American action at this time.

In the presence of the Joint Chiefs, Kennedy again apologized for delaying any attack and thus complicating military preparations. Rusk caught his drift and said pointedly that anyone who thought the planned action was "weak" should know that "in a number of hours we'll have a flaming crisis on our hands."

What then were the "dirty" questions the government would face?

Why didn't Kennedy act sooner? The group agreed to say that without firm evidence of "offensive" weapons, there would have been no support from either Latin or European allies. Then, too, the earlier reports from Cuban refugees did not constitute reliable "surveillance." (Analysts later showed that the U-2s might have discovered the missiles in late September, or three weeks sooner, if they had not been barred from flying across the island.)

Why not take stronger action immediately? Bundy warned against talking about the difficulty of hitting all targets when they might well want to try hitting them soon enough. Rusk suggested citing an obligation to first take the issue to the United Nations and OAS. Most of all, however, Kennedy wanted to hide the truth—that doubt about defending Berlin had stayed his hand. He was in fact deterred by the fear of a nuclear exchange, but that was not something he cared to admit. He preferred to tell the world that his restraint was rooted in moral concerns. He asked Robert Kennedy to keep stressing what he called "the Pearl Harbor defense," the desire not to initiate a deadly surprise attack, and Bobby faithfully honored that wish, to his dying day.

The toughest question, in Kennedy's view, was why he considered the Soviet missiles in Cuba to be different from America's missiles in Turkey and Italy. His unsatisfying answer was that the U.S. missiles were installed openly, to balance Soviet missiles targeted on Western Europe, whereas the Soviet deployment was secret and threatened to strengthen communism in our hemisphere. As his readiness to trade away the Jupiters made clear, the president did not really respect this part of his argument.

Someone asked whether the quarantine covered air cargoes, and they decided to remain vague about that. Was there now a national emergency? No, but there could be any hour, should be the answer. Will all ships be stopped or only Soviet-bloc vessels? They would say all, although in fact they had not yet chosen any.

"All right," the president interrupted, suddenly returning to his real concern about public comment. "I don't want to leave this dangling. . . . I think we've got an agreement about what our status is re invasion: 'No orders for that have been given.' I've only said we'd be prepared for that eventuality."

"Right," said McNamara.

As for air action, Kennedy reiterated, he did not want to betray his fear of Soviet counteraction. "I can't say that strongly enough—we don't want to ever have it around that this was one of the alternatives that we considered this week. . . . I do think it's vitally important that we not discuss the tactical nature or the strategic nature of it and stick with the Pearl Harbor explanation" for not immediately attacking Cuba.

After briefing his cabinet along similar lines and receiving the prime minister of Uganda, Kennedy moved to the most difficult chore of a difficult day. He confronted twenty leaders of Congress who had been ferried from all corners of the country by military transport. They were pleased to be informed, but resentful to be only consulted. Among them sat Senators Richard Russell and J. William Fulbright, the most influential Democrats on military and foreign affairs; Senator Everett Dirksen, the Republican leader; and several leaders of the House. Conspicuously omitted was the Cassandra of the crisis, Senator Keating.

McCone and his aides recited their discoveries, adding the news that the bases were manned entirely by Soviets and that some of the radars of their SAM antiaircraft units had now begun to latch on to the U-2 spy planes flying overhead. Thompson recalled his last meeting with Khrushchev in July, which led him to conclude that the Soviet leader intended in November to use the Cuban deployment to bargain for a new status for Berlin and East Germany. The president, faced with intense questioning from the legislators about why he did not attack the missile sites, repeated his concerns about a "very strong" Soviet response in Europe. If the missiles were not removed, he would next consider extending the boycott of Cuba to bar petroleum and other products, except perhaps food and medicine.

Senator Russell pressed for invasion: "We're either a first-class power or we're not." Though he did not really think it likely, the president replied that an invasion would risk having the missiles fired at the United States. Senator Fulbright favored invasion for a different reason—to confront Cuban rather than Soviet power. The president took Thompson's view that killing several thousand Russians from the air would be worse than stopping their ships. Although upset by this congressional dissent, Kennedy soon realized that the reactions were no more belligerent than his own first instincts six long days before.

"Bullfight critics, row on row . . ." But only one who fights the bull.

Nikita Khrushchev
greets a new friend,
in Harlem, 1960.

And a new adversary,
in Vienna, 1961.

And plots the missile ploy
with Marshal Malinovsky,
in 1962.

MRBM FIELD LAUNCH SITE
SAN CRISTOBAL NO 1
14 OCTOBER 1962

ERECTOR/LAUNCHER EQUIPMENT

TENT AREAS

EQUIPMENT

ERECTOR/LAUNCHER EQUIPMENT

8 MISSILE TRAILERS

CONSTRUCTION

4

Washington's first proof of missiles arriving in Cuba, as photographed by a U-2.

MRBM LAUNCH SITE 1
SAN CRISTOBAL, CUBA
23 OCTOBER 1962

MISSILE ERECTOR

CABLE

MISSILE SHELTER TENT

TRACKED PRIME MOVERS

FUEL TANK TRAILERS

OXIDIZER TANK TRAILERS

5

The same base nine days later, after President Kennedy demanded its removal.

6
Oval Office minuet: Gromyko lies, and Kennedy pretends to believe him.

7
Presidential aria: Kennedy springs a surprise and invites a diplomatic duel.

Gray, grave, and without makeup, the president invoked "the abyss" of nuclear destruction on Oct. 22, 1962.

8

9

And schoolchildren practiced "duck and cover" routines in vulnerable Florida.

10

11

Two typical views of ExCom at work. The standees are Robert Kennedy at left and Secretary Dean Rusk beside the president.

12

On the White House portico, beyond the range of hidden microphones:
National Security Adviser McGeorge Bundy; President Kennedy;
General Maxwell Taylor, and Defense Secretary Robert McNamara.

The ExCom
inside ExCom:
Brothers Bobby
and Jack.

13

14

President Kennedy was only stiffly aligned with his Pentagon team—on his right, Generals Shoup and Wheeler, Admiral Anderson and Secretary McNamara; on his left, General Taylor, Deputy Secretary Gilpatric, and General LeMay.

The president had wide public support, but protesters marched at the UN and also on many campuses.

15

16

Inside the UN, the U.S. delegate, Adlai Stevenson, mocked the denials of Ambassador Zorin (at left) with photos of the missiles.

President Kennedy declaring the crisis formally ended on Nov. 2, 1962.

17

18

Not until ten months after the crisis, at his Black Sea villa, did Khrushchev—seated between Gromyko and Dobrynin—pose the ultimate question to the round-faced Rusk, sitting beside Ambassador Thompson, near right.

EIGHT

AND WHO WILL BLINK?

D URING MONDAY, OCTOBER 22, THE TENSIONS BUILDING
in Washington finally registered in Moscow. So did the sus-
pense about a mysterious "crisis" generated by vague American news
reports that morning. Berlin and Germany were obviously calm.
What then was agitating the White House? Obviously, the Russians
concluded, their missiles had been discovered. And since the rockets
were not armed with nuclear warheads, would the Americans attack?

"They are defenseless and everything could be destroyed from the
air at one blow," Khrushchev remarked to his son, Sergei. Worse still,
the American ships massing in the Caribbean seemed to be preparing
an invasion. And Fidel Castro was mobilizing. What if at any moment
he wanted Soviet troops to help defend the island? Were Russians and
Americans close to war?

Even in a crisis of his own making, Khrushchev's instincts, like
Kennedy's, ran to prudence. He quickly ordered General Pliyev in
Havana to make ready to "repulse the enemy together with the
Cuban army" with all his forces—*except nuclear weapons*. Though

tough in tone, this message was actually restraining. It had the effect of rescinding a standing order that Pliyev might, in extremis, fire his twelve nuclear artillery shells on his own authority if Americans invaded and he had lost all contact with Moscow. The new orders meant that without Khrushchev's explicit consent, nuclear weapons were not to be used under any circumstances.[13]

By early evening in Moscow, the Russians learned that Kennedy would speak on American television at 2 AM (7 PM in Washington) on "a matter of the highest national urgency." Sizing up the moment for Sergei, Khrushchev doubted that Kennedy would be giving advance notice if he planned to attack. He guessed, and hoped, that the president would rather bargain than fight.

But Khrushchev also understood that he had suddenly lost the initiative in Cuba.

Grimly, he summoned his Presidium to a night session to sweat out Kennedy's first move. Fear creased their faces, but none of the communist oligarchs dared now to second-guess their leader; the Cuba venture had been Khrushchev's inspiration, and they would leave it to him to cope with the consequences. Marshal Malinovsky tried to lift his commander's spirits by suggesting that the Kennedy broadcast might be a "pre-election trick" rather than a serious challenge. Khrushchev knew better.

"We missed our chance," he told the marshal, meaning they had failed to protect their secret past the volatile American election season. He seemed to Sergei to be regretting his failure to deploy all the

---

[13] A possibly related reaction was the arrest in Moscow that very day of Colonel Oleg Penkovsky, whom the KGB had previously spotted as a spy for the West. He had revealed enough about Soviet missiles to help identify those in Cuba. It was bruited years later that as he was dragged off toward summary execution Penkovsky sent the wrong prearranged signal to Americans, warning not of his imminent arrest but of an imminent Soviet attack on the United States. The CIA was said to have quickly discounted this alarm without even alerting the White House. But the anecdote is often cited as one of the fluke events that could have made a tense situation even worse.

weapons at once, and especially his decision to hold back missile-firing submarines that would by now have reached American waters and reinforced his diplomacy. Sergei also thought his father regretted not publishing a treaty proclaiming a Soviet commitment to Cuba's defense, as Castro had urged.

All these regrets dissolved into relief when, after midnight, Ambassador Dobrynin flashed a summary of the Kennedy text given him by Secretary Rusk.[14] The worst had not happened. That curiously named "quarantine" was a nasty challenge, of course; a blockade by any name was an act of war. But it was not—yet—an attack.

There was time to see what could be salvaged from a bad situation. Khrushchev decided that the four attack submarines should proceed to protect the four ships carrying intermediate-range missiles. And the *Aleksandrovsk*, packed with nuclear warheads for the IRBMs and for coastal defense weapons, could still slip into a Cuban port before the quarantine took effect. Perhaps daylight would reveal brighter opportunities. Khrushchev urged his colleagues to stay the night in the Kremlin so that American agents and journalists would not detect any nervousness. "Let them think we're peacefully asleep in our beds," he said.

In the same low-key spirit, the Soviet armed forces were ordered to increase "combat readiness and vigilance," a fairly modest alert compared with the ostentatious American preparations that the Pentagon wanted the Russians to observe.

Kennedy that day invoked Defense Condition 3 (DEFCON-1 was for war). The most visible effect was to send sixty-six nuclear-armed bombers, instead of the normal twelve, on flight paths toward the Soviet Union, menacingly ready for further orders. The Pentagon also

---

[14] "Dobrynin aged at least ten years right before my eyes," Rusk remembered years later. "He reacted as a man in physical shock. 'This is a terrible situation,' he said. 'A most unfortunate thing for us to do.'" The secretary of state assumed, correctly, that the ambassador had not been told about the missile deployment and had been denying it, as ordered, in good faith.

alerted domestic railroads to help move five army divisions and one of marines to Florida and Georgia. The navy sent 180 vessels into the Caribbean, including eight aircraft carriers, plotted the position of all Cuba-bound ships, and prepared to join with the air force to fly one thousand attack sorties against Cuba on a single day. In full view of the Cubans, the navy evacuated twenty-five hundred women and children from Guantánamo, in such haste that many husbands and fathers never got to say good-bye.

Equally belligerent—and intentionally alarmist—were Kennedy's words as he appeared, grave and gray, without makeup, before a hundred million Americans, the largest television audience to that time.

The president denounced the "secret, swift and extraordinary" buildup in Cuba, noting that it had occurred "in violation of Soviet assurances." He listed Khrushchev's falsehoods, then summarized his grievance: "This sudden, clandestine decision to station strategic weapons for the first time outside of Soviet soil is a deliberately provocative and unjustified change in the status quo, which cannot be accepted by this country if our courage and our commitments are ever to be trusted again by either friend or foe."

His objective, Kennedy asserted, was to prevent the use of the missiles and then to secure "their withdrawal or elimination."

To rattle Soviet nerves, Kennedy's speech had to scare people everywhere: "We will not prematurely or unnecessarily risk the costs of worldwide nuclear war in which even the fruits of victory would be ashes in our mouth—but neither will we shrink from that risk at any time it must be faced." The president threatened a still tighter blockade if needed and "further action" beyond that if the military work in Cuba continued. Most solemnly, he warned that any missile launched from Cuba would be considered an attack by the Soviet Union on the United States, requiring a full retaliatory response. Any hostile move elsewhere, especially against Berlin, would be met "by whatever action is needed." Only a Soviet withdrawal could "move the world back from the abyss of destruction."

Conditioned for years to believe that the Soviet Union was hell-bent on conquering the world for communism, a great many Americans concluded that the day of reckoning had arrived. They rushed to hoard food and gasoline. Some reminded schoolchildren how to duck under desks to avoid the fallout from nuclear explosions. The few who had heeded Kennedy's prior advice to build backyard fallout shelters checked on their condition. Most Americans expected a long and tense period of crisis and possible conflict. They took to heart the president's prediction that they faced "many months" of sacrifice with unpredictable "costs or casualties." The anxiety they felt that night lingered long in the minds of all who heard Kennedy's speech.

But "the greatest danger of all," the president insisted, "would be to do nothing."

PORTENDING THE MANY FRUSTRATING, now dangerous communication delays between capitals whose clocks stood seven hours apart,[15] Ambassador Kohler had to search hard in the middle of the Moscow night for someone to receive a secret supplementary letter from Kennedy to Khrushchev. It expressed particular concern that the Soviet leader would underestimate "the will and determination of the United States"—meaning, of course, the will and determination of the president. The quarantine was the "minimum" action necessary to remove the threat to American security, Kennedy wrote. But he did not want that minimal choice to cause "any misjudgment on your part."

Kennedy spoke still more ominously in a call to Britain's Prime Minister Macmillan, no doubt hoping that a relayed (or purloined) account of their conversation would further add to the pressure on Khrushchev. While Macmillan urged negotiation, the president

---

[15] The difference became eight hours with Washington's shift to Eastern Standard Time on October 28.

stressed danger. He said he planned to escalate his actions gradually, to reduce "the chance of a seizure of Berlin or World War III." But: "We may not prevent either."

KHRUSHCHEV SOON UNDERSTOOD THAT Kennedy had produced a brew of dire threat and prudent action. This encouraged him to stall for time with a similar mix. He, too, could play on the world's anxiety, reiterating references to the "abyss" of nuclear war while in fact offering to negotiate. His monopoly over the Soviet media offered the chance to exacerbate fears abroad without confessing that he had led the Russian people to the edge of war. Throughout the crisis, the Soviet press and radio never once mentioned "nuclear missiles" as the source of the trouble over Cuba.

Indeed, the Soviet government's first public statement, though vitriolic, pretended that the United States had challenged not the Soviet Union but innocent, harmless Cuba. It denounced the blockade as piracy and "a step along the road of unleashing a thermonuclear world war." It argued that the removal of "military equipment that Cuba needs" for defense was a demand that no self-respecting state could honor. It vowed to protect Cuba, yet promised to preserve the peace and looked mainly to the United Nations for help and support.

Khrushchev also understood that Kennedy's private letter amounted to an invitation to begin direct negotiations. And he responded in kind. He acknowledged in his secret reply that the president's "aggressive actions" were aimed at the Soviet Union as well as Cuba. But he argued that the "armaments now on Cuba," no matter what their classification, were "destined exclusively for defensive purposes." He asked Kennedy to avoid "catastrophe" by canceling the blockade.

Because Khrushchev's fulminations lacked any clear threat of counteraction, American analysts immediately saw them as a holding action, a sign of indecision or even confusion. But Castro lacked their experience in parsing Soviet rhetoric and, as intended, misread the Soviet leader's meaning. In writing to Fidel, Khrushchev denounced the "pirate-like, perfidious and aggressive actions" of the United States. He expressed "determination to fight actively against such actions" and described Soviet forces as "completely ready for combat." Actually, however, Khrushchev promised nothing more than a vigorous protest at the UN. Wrongly but understandably, Castro thought he had received a Soviet commitment to fight at Cuba's side. He clearly remembered, decades later, telling colleagues without particular remorse, "Well, it looks like war. I cannot conceive of any retreat." As a close associate observed years later, "Don't forget, Fidel gets his kicks from war and high tension. He can't stand not being front-page news."

TUESDAY, OCTOBER 23, was a good day for the Kennedy team. The American people were remarkably trusting of their government, even though three of five people expected some shooting to occur and one of five expected it to result in a "world war." Not many of those polled, however, feared a nuclear war. The president himself briefly wondered what he might do to reduce civilian casualties if the worst occurred but concluded that the panic caused by such preparations was not worth the modest benefits to be gained.

Kennedy came to work smiling on Tuesday morning. So did Rusk, who greeted the dawn at the State Department by telling Undersecretary Ball that "we've won a great victory—you and I are still alive." What they were all celebrating, in yet another official's phrase, was that "we really caught them with their contingencies down."

As intended, the Russians were surprised and off-balance. As no one in ExCom expected, they were also unprepared with any significant response. Washington's all-night intelligence vigil had found no disturbing Soviet troop movements anywhere. And reassuringly, only Russians were seen commanding the missile sites in Cuba. Though he

had been outmaneuvered, Khrushchev seemed intent to hold his fire
and to keep talking.

In fact, the chairman's dejection was greater than the ExCom
knew. When one of his aides took up Dobrynin's suggestion that they
retaliate by blocking American access to West Berlin, Khrushchev
shot back harshly: "Keep that kind of advice to yourself. We don't
know how to get out of one predicament and you drag us into another!"[16]

More good news soon reached the White House from the Organization of American States, down the street. Normally reticent Latin
nations were willing this time to invoke the Rio Treaty to authorize
"all measures necessary" to remove a Soviet threat to the hemisphere.
At Thompson's urging, Kennedy had delayed the start of the quarantine to wait for that legal cover to impress the Soviets. The mood in
ExCom became so bubbly that members burst into mocking laughter
when told that Marshal Malinovsky had ordered "no further demobi-
lization of forces."

In this relaxed moment, Kennedy showed as much concern about
Senator Keating as Chairman Khrushchev. He asked John McCone
to meet with congressional hawks and to testify to the president's
toughness even as he himself cautioned the navy to restrain its conduct in the Caribbean. The president was sure the Russians would not
risk interception and capture of their nuclear missiles, so he wanted to
guard against any provocative confrontation at the designated line of
quarantine, the Q-line. He even asked that sailors be required to surrender personal cameras so that they could not record any Soviet humiliation or, indeed, American embarrassment. As he put it, he did
not want some merchant ship shot at and towed to port only to find
that it was carrying baby food. McNamara was itching to chase any

---

[16] Most of the direct quotes here and later from the Kremlin councils come from
Oleg Troyanovsky, Khrushchev's foreign affairs aide, who wrote and spoke ex-
tensively about the crisis in later years.

retreating vessels to get some close-up photos of secret Soviet equipment, but the president forbad it. Low-level aerial reconnaissance over Cuba would suffice to gather evidence for the skeptics at the UN and in the British press.

SWORDS CROSSED, both Khrushchev and Kennedy tried on Wednesday, October 24, to pressure each other while taking care to avoid a clash.

The Soviets worked around the clock to finish assembly of the unloaded missile launchers, belatedly hiding or camouflaging some of them. Kennedy accelerated his visible preparations for air attacks and amphibious landings. But the president and the chairman also exchanged gentler signals. Even in his denunciation of the Russians at the UN, Stevenson showed himself ready to enter discussions. And Tuesday evening, Khrushchev led half his Presidium to a performance of *Boris Godunov,* at the end of which he sought out Jerome Hines, the American basso, and praised his portrayal of the Russian czar. The cordiality implicit in that gesture harked back to June, when Kennedy privately thanked Khrushchev for attending a Moscow concert by Benny Goodman and declared himself eager to welcome the Bolshoi Ballet to Washington in the fall.

More signals were passed by Robert Kennedy through Georgi Bolshakov, the Soviet agent who had taxed their relationship by lying about the Cuban buildup. Bobby still kept him at arm's length, but he sent two friends in the Washington press corps to tell Bolshakov that a withdrawal of the missiles might, in calmer days, be reciprocated with an American withdrawal of the Jupiters from Turkey. The president's hand has never been detected in this suggestion, but Bobby well knew that his voice carried presidential weight in Moscow.

A similar desire to turn any negotiation away from Berlin and to direct it toward Turkey instead was conveyed through my reporting by obviously well-informed White House sources. Their message still lingers conspicuously on the front page of *The New York Times* of October 24, 1962, in an article that included this prominent point:

> The Western position in Berlin, officials insist, is not negotiable. . . . However, some sources said that if the Russians wished to engage in negotiations for the dismantling of offensive missile bases in Cuba, it was conceivable that the United States might be willing to dismantle one of the obsolescent American bases near Soviet territory. . . .
>
> The Administration does not concede the Soviet argument that missile bases in Turkey or on the soil of other Western military allies are comparable to Soviet bases in Cuba. But it is mindful of the appeal of this argument and of the possibility that the Soviet counter-move will be aimed at these allies.[17]

Having offered an olive branch in the afternoon, Bobby threw daggers in a late-night visit to the Soviet embassy. Ambassador Dobrynin remembered him arriving in "an agitated state" to urge that Cuba-bound vessels turn back without challenging the quarantine. The ambassador thought the younger Kennedy "was far from being a sociable person" and lacking a sense of humor. But the visit opened yet another vital channel of communication.

By presidential proclamation, the quarantine was declared effective Wednesday morning at ten o'clock Washington time. But it became a very fluid quarantine along a shifting line, allowing Kennedy and Khrushchev to let their ships weave and bob away from confrontation.

Gestures dominated the game. Also at 10 AM, the Strategic Air Command sent out uncoded messages that raised the alert of its nu-

---

[17] The article was headlined, "U.S. Sees Moscow Caught Off Guard. Believes Blockade of Cuba Has Interrupted Move to Force Terms on Berlin." The names of my informants, alas, are long forgotten.

clear forces another notch, to DEFCON-2, one step below all-out war. The Soviets, in turn, made a show of refusing to receive the "rules" for naval contact at the quarantine line. The line itself was moved by Kennedy, on the advice of his friend Ambassador Ormsby-Gore of Britain, to a point five hundred miles from Cuba, instead of eight hundred, so as to buy another few hours before it was reached by the next Soviet ship. Urgent coded messages from Moscow seemed to be sending new instructions to most of the Cuba-bound vessels, but Washington could not immediately decipher them.

Kennedy's gravest moment on Wednesday morning came with the news that a Soviet submarine was escorting two Soviet cargo ships only an hour from the Q-line. The navy boasted that it could safely force the sub to surface with harmless, "practice" depth charges and that it could stop merchant ships, if necessary, by crippling their rudders. But the president peered beyond the horizon. If a Soviet ship were sunk, he said, "there would be a blockade" in Berlin; "then we would be faced with ordering air in there, which is probably going to be shot down, which is—what is then our situation? What do we do then?"

What all of ExCom did then was turn to CIA director McCone, who announced abruptly that six Soviet ships had stopped in mid-ocean or actually reversed course. Were they ships headed *toward* Cuba? The note handed him was unclear; he had to check. Minutes later he learned that yes, they really were ships sailing toward Cuba with suspect cargoes of weapons and related equipment. The room shook with excitement because as someone finally realized, Khrushchev was respecting—tacitly *accepting*—the blockade.

"We are eyeball to eyeball and I think the other fellow just blinked," Rusk whispered to Bundy. To the broader meeting, Rusk quickly added that the navy had better be instructed to avoid all interceptions pending new orders. Mere minutes after the quarantine took effect, both sides were backing away from confrontation at sea.

. . .

AS KENNEDY HAD PREDICTED, the Russians were making sure to keep their major weapons out of American hands. But more than a dozen other cargo ships were still Cuba-bound, and if his embargo were to remain credible, he would have to inspect something sometime. A Soviet tanker, the *Bucharest*, was to reach the Q-line before dawn Thursday. If allowed to pass while nothing else occurred, the Soviets would continue to build the missile bases and then negotiate with new strength to keep them in place.

Kennedy now faced what he always knew to be the weakness of the quarantine. It alone could not compel removal of the missiles. If construction continued, the United States might have to shoot first after all and risk a violent Soviet response in Europe.

And although he flinched at sea, Khrushchev was not yet pulling out of Cuba. On Wednesday afternoon in Moscow, he summoned William Knox, an American businessman whom he must have considered a secret agent, to deliver a three-hour lecture and message to Washington. The nuclear missiles in Cuba were strictly for defense, he insisted, all under his personal control, never to be fired first. Now leave our ships alone! Sometimes people just had to learn to live with a smelly goat in the house. Russians were living with a lot of smelly Western goats in neighboring countries. To calm the situation, Khrushchev offered to meet Kennedy anywhere. But "if the United States insists on war, we'll all meet in hell."

A follow-up letter to Kennedy veered close to insult. Khrushchev denounced the quarantine as an unacceptable "ultimatum" born not only of hatred for Cubans but also of cynical American election politics. Still rattling his rockets, Khrushchev said the president must know that the United States has "fully lost its former inaccessibility." He could not possibly order Soviet seamen to obey American orders. He would defend his ships as necessary.

"It looks really mean, doesn't it?" the president remarked to brother Bobby. "But then, really, there was no other choice. If they get this mean on this one [crisis] in our part of the world, what will they do on the next?" Foreign and domestic politics struck the brothers as inseparable. "If you hadn't acted you would have been impeached," said Bobby. Jack Kennedy wistfully agreed.

Still looking to drag out the diplomacy, Khrushchev turned to U Thant, the acting secretary-general of the UN, to have him propose a suspension of "aggravating" actions for two or three weeks. Kennedy finessed this idea. He would suspend the quarantine only if the UN were allowed to inspect the cargoes reaching Cuba, which itself would take days to arrange. He offered to let the tanker *Bucharest* sail unmolested past the Q-line if Khrushchev held back other cargo ships for a day or two so that diplomats could confer.

Keeping hands off the *Bucharest* and other Soviet vessels was no simple matter. To gain control of the action at sea, Kennedy asked McNamara to monitor all navy plans. There was to be no shooting at rudders or other use of force without the secretary's permission, was that clear?

Smarting under this White House interference, Admiral Anderson argued that he sure knew how to run a blockade, by the book, without the secretary's help, thank you. Regulations covering a blockade, he said, were as old as the navy.

"I don't give a damn what John Paul Jones would have done," McNamara replied. "I want to know what you are going to do—now." The president's objective with this quarantine, the secretary lectured, was to send "a political message," not to start a war.

To his deputy, McNamara fumed, "That's the end of Anderson."[18]

---

[18] The admiral quickly calmed down and acknowledged McNamara's authority. Soon after the crisis, however, he was exiled to be ambassador to Portugal. (See Shapley, Deborah. *Promise and Power: The Life and Times of Robert McNamara.* Boston: Little, Brown, 1994.)

. . .

IT WAS NOT, HOWEVER, the end of Wednesday night's fateful exchanges.

At Washington's National Press Club, a Russian immigrant tending bar well after midnight overheard Warren Rogers of *The New York Herald Tribune* tell his bureau chief, Robert Donovan, about the Pentagon's stand-by arrangements for taking reporters along on any invasion of Cuba. Within hours, that barroom gossip was being processed at the Soviet embassy, presumed to be a reliable clue that an invasion was due in a day or two. Soviet agents even contrived to bump into Rogers Thursday morning; they engaged him in conversation and misinterpreted his references to a determined president as confirmation that an attack was imminent.

Coincidentally, Thursday's *Herald Tribune* carried a much more meaningful view of the crisis for all the world to read. After a conversation with Undersecretary of State George Ball and probably also with Bundy, the capital's foremost columnist, Walter Lippmann, delivered the opinion that the "defenseless" Soviet bases in Cuba were comparable to America's "obsolete" Jupiter bases in Turkey. Both sets of bases were provocative and ineffectual, he wrote, and they "could be dismantled without altering the world balance of power."

Kennedy knew that the Soviets would read Lippmann's column as an authorized trial balloon for a deal and he told associates the proposal was "premature." But even if mistimed, the idea of mutual base withdrawals already hung in the Washington air. Rusk had even asked Ambassador Raymond Hare in Turkey how such a deal might be arranged without wrecking relations with an important ally.

AS HE LET THE *BUCHAREST* PASS the Q-line, Kennedy sent a curt reply to Khrushchev's threat to keep sending his ships toward Cuba. He did not start this crisis, Kennedy wrote, and the Soviet leader had better recognize his own culpability. The president recalled assurances, public and private, that no offensive weapons were being sent to Cuba. Relying on those assurances, "I urged restraint upon those in this country who were urging action. . . . And then I learned beyond doubt what you have not denied—namely, that all these public assurances were false." The president closed with regrets for the tension in relations; he hoped Khrushchev would "take the necessary action to permit a restoration of the earlier situation."

A growing complication in this secret correspondence was that events threatened to outrun the mails. The two capitals shared only half a dozen hours of daylight, and a message to Moscow could take six or more hours to reach its destination. As the Soviet ambassador in Washington remembered, his cables home had to be painstakingly coded into columns of numbers, then handed to a Western Union messenger on a bicycle. "Usually it was the same young black man," Dobrynin remembered, and the ambassador could only hope the cyclist would not stop "to chat on the way with some girl." (Telephones were quicker but scorned by diplomats as too easily overheard. Then again, no one has ever explained why the Kennedy–Khrushchev exchanges had to be encoded when delay was surely a greater danger than Chinese or French eavesdropping.)

WHEN IT FINALLY REACHED MOSCOW on Thursday, October 25, Kennedy's cool response gave Khrushchev a surprisingly warm feeling. The chairman said the letter made him lose interest in more "caustic" exchanges with the president. Sergei Khrushchev remembered thinking that his father was "touched" by the letter's closing appeal for better relations.

Touching but implausible. The Soviet leader was not one to be unhorsed by platitudes or empty promises. There is no doubt, however, that he came to the Kremlin Thursday resolved to end the crisis quickly, cut his losses, and salvage what he could for his reputation as a statesman.

What really turned him so fast? He may have been scared, intimidated to some degree by the global alert of America's nuclear forces. He may also have been encouraged to bargain by Kennedy's obvious reluctance to attack the Soviet bases or even stop a Soviet vessel. Khrushchev must have realized that he would not fare well in any confrontation so far from home against America's overwhelming local strength. And nothing gained in Cuba could justify attacking Americans in Europe and triggering a major war. Khrushchev had recognized from the start that he had probably lost his gamble to finish the deployment in secret, and over the past forty-eight hours he had hit upon a path of retreat that might yet allow him to claim some success.

Khrushchev told his Presidium that he had decided to withdraw the missiles from Cuba provided Kennedy promised in turn not to invade the island. Then, to verify the withdrawal and to protect Fidel Castro, he would let the UN police Cuba as a "zone of peace." Only days earlier, in his conversation with Gromyko, Kennedy had twice offered to pay the very price that Khrushchev was now requesting. The president had described the Cuban arms buildup as entirely unnecessary because he "would have been glad to give appropriate assurances" that there would be "no further invasion, either by refugees or by U.S. forces"—if only Khrushchev had asked.

Well now, better late than never, the Soviet leader would ask. And he would tell the world that his missile maneuver had rescued the Castro revolution from certain destruction by the imperialists.

Some Presidium members were surely shocked to learn, as was his son, Sergei, that Khrushchev would trust a mere promise by Kennedy not to invade Cuba again. Sergei remembered his father's incisive response: "Once you begin shooting, you can't stop." There was no better way out.

Still, having designed a deal that he was sure he could get, Khrushchev decided there was time for his diplomats and agents to "look around" to gain a sense of Kennedy's receptivity and to learn what else might be achieved.

. . .

IN WASHINGTON, HOWEVER, Thursday passed with no real hint of Khrushchev's new flexibility. Kennedy and the ExCom strained to devise measures and messages that in combination would continue to appear both tough and reasonable.

At 7 AM, a U.S. destroyer asked the *Bucharest* to identify herself and her cargo and, when she complied, let the tanker proceed under surveillance. Castro staged a jubilant welcome, celebrating "defeat" of the blockade. In an annoyed rebuttal, the Pentagon boasted that at least a dozen Cuba-bound ships had turned tail and that the *Bucharest* had been "intercepted and permitted to proceed." Later Thursday, Kennedy ordered hands off an East German ship carrying fifteen hundred soldier-passengers. That bought thirty more hours for diplomacy until the next vessel, another tanker, reached the U.S. cordon.

Rusk and McNamara designed parallel gestures that balanced diplomacy with shows of force. The defense secretary won Kennedy's consent to send fighter planes roaring over the missile bases at altitudes of less than a thousand feet. Their mission was to gather intelligence, but they also simulated bombing runs; that would assure surprise if they ever actually meant to bomb. And if still more menace was wanted, McNamara said, he could order night flights with flares, producing a "really quite startling" effect, and he could devise other "harassing action." Rusk meanwhile kept deflecting U Thant's bid for a fortnight's "pause" in the quarantine, insisting that "the answer lies in the removal" of the Soviet missiles. The United States agreed to preliminary UN talks provided Soviet ships avoided the Q-line and UN inspectors were able to "defang" the completed missile bases. Rusk also expressed interest in a Brazilian proposal to declare all Latin America off-limits to nuclear weapons. And he toyed briefly with the thought of trying to use the moment to lure Castro away from his Soviet patrons. This strange idea was probably inspired by the fact that clear through the crisis, the Cubans continued to negotiate in Havana with James B. Donovan, a New York lawyer sent by the CIA to ransom the eleven hundred Cuban exiles who were taken prisoner at the Bay of Pigs. (The price, finally fixed in December, became fifty-three million dollars' worth of food and medicine.)

The Soviet ambassador in Havana, meanwhile, reported that the Cuban leaders were calm and businesslike, notably lacking their usual "ostentation and verbosity." Castro had endorsed Khrushchev's decision to avoid conflict by having some vessels turn around. But he wanted to shoot down "one or two of the piratic U.S. planes" that were now scaring his population from the treetops. Noting that the Soviet SAMs could not deal with low-flying aircraft, Fidel was delighted to find a role for himself and his forces. He deployed fifty Cuban antiaircraft guns around the Soviet installations and warned that he would no longer tolerate the frightening American reconnaissance runs. At the same time, he reassured the Soviets by telling them that he gave little credit to his "unverifiable information" that the United States planned to attack Cuba on Friday or Saturday.

Much of the "intelligence" reaching all three governments was by now not very intelligent. In cables from Washington, Ambassador Dobrynin relayed the misleading gossip from the National Press Club bar and an equally wrong report that Robert Kennedy and Mc-Namara were eagerly urging an attack on Cuba. And the ill-briefed Soviet ambassador at the UN, Valerian Zorin, was still denying the missile deployments when Adlai Stevenson produced photos of them before the television cameras and offered scrappily to wait for a Soviet acknowledgment "until hell freezes over."

Stevenson's tough turn in the Security Council surprised Kennedy, who went to bed Thursday pleased with the balance he had achieved. He felt he could now afford to let another Soviet tanker pass unmolested without appearing weak. To make a show of finally intercepting a vessel, he had selected the *Marucla*, an American-built Liberty ship, Panamanian owned, which was sailing under Lebanese registry, Greek command, and Soviet charter and due to reach the

Q-line on Friday. The president planned then to wait for U Thant or Khrushchev to devise a promising offer while he continued the reconnaissance flights over Cuba and his loud complaints about the still feverish work at the missile sites.

If the Soviets held firm, the president had virtually decided that "the obvious escalation" would be to add petroleum products to the embargo list, which would slowly cripple both Cuban and Soviet operations on the island. In his nightly call to Prime Minister Macmillan, he said his first objective now was to get Khrushchev to announce a suspension of arms shipments, then make him stop work at the missile bases and, if refused, tighten the blockade. Thinking—or posturing—far ahead as well, Kennedy also told the CIA to plan for a new Cuban government if he should ever decide to invade.

The first reliable clue that a tighter blockade or use of force might not be necessary was set in type Thursday night in the offices of *Pravda*, the Soviet Communist party newspaper, whose articles routinely served Khrushchev's propaganda and policy interests. Wednesday morning, in its first response to Kennedy's challenge, the paper ran a ranting headline: THE UNLEASHED AMERICAN AGGRESSORS MUST BE STOPPED! HANDS OFF CUBA! Pravda was still screaming for blood with Thursday's banner: THE AGGRESSIVE DESIGNS OF UNITED STATES IMPERIALISTS MUST BE FOILED. PEACE ON EARTH MUST BE DEFENDED AND STRENGTHENED! But the Friday paper turned temperate. It tamely announced: EVERYTHING TO PREVENT WAR and offered an editorial titled REASON MUST PREVAIL.

THE STARS SEEMED ALIGNED. It could have been, should have been, a very good Friday.

Khrushchev's agents went forth, as instructed, to test his terms for a deal. They hoped, at first, that the chairman would not have to reveal himself as the sponsor of his own retreat. By midmorning, U Thant had been encouraged to offer Khrushchev's bargain as his own—a missile withdrawal in exchange for a no-invasion pledge. Almost simultaneously, the same idea appeared as the invention of Canadian diplomats. And at noon in Washington, the KGB chief urgently asked his occasional lunch partner, John Scali of ABC News, to solicit an official reaction to the identical formula, which he called his own. By the time Scali returned with a show of interest, however, these maneuvers were already overtaken by Khrushchev's direct diplomacy.

For its part, the Kennedy team began Friday with the desire to prove at least once that it had the courage of its own blockade. At 8 AM, just as John Paul Jones would have directed, unarmed naval officers in dress whites from the destroyers *Pierce* and *Joseph Kennedy* (conveniently bearing the name of the president's late brother) climbed aboard the *Marucla*, whose captain had been primed for these theatrics. The Americans read his manifests over Greek coffee, then searched a dozen trucks on deck, inspected rolls of paper and barrels of sulfur below, opened a crate labeled PRECISION INSTRUMENTS, and courteously waved the vessel on. Virility asserted, the president had no more desire to bother a Swedish freighter that churned past the Q-line Friday afternoon, even though it refused the navy's order to stop.

Kennedy was focused now on all the Soviet feelers about a no-invasion guarantee. Such a pledge had never figured in his calculations about how the crisis might end, but he embraced the idea without hesitation. "If that's one of the prices that has to be paid to get these [missiles] out of there, then we commit ourselves not to invade Cuba," he said. "We weren't going to invade them anyway." Rusk, too, was quick to rationalize a no-invasion promise as no real concession because, he said, Cuba already enjoyed the protection of the UN Charter and Rio Treaty. Besides, the president observed, nothing in diplomacy was forever. If invading Cuba ever became desirable—or necessary to avenge a move against Berlin—he could always say, "This changes our commitments."

Just as Khrushchev was hoping to hide his authorship of the deal, Kennedy hoped to disguise his acceptance. He wondered whether the no-invasion pledge could be given not by the United States but collectively, by the Organization of American States. In just a few more hours, however, both Kennedy and Khrushchev overcame their reticence and owned up to their eagerness to escape the crisis.

Kennedy still wondered whether diplomacy alone could really get the missiles out of Cuba; the Russians were working too hard to finish the bases. But he was clear in his own mind about the stark choice ahead. He kept telling associates, "We're either going to trade them out or we're going to have to go in and get them out ourselves."

And if diplomacy still looked bleak, invasion looked bleaker. McCone now brought detailed pictures of the Soviet bases, which prompted Kennedy to observe that by the time American troops waged "a very bloody fight" to reach them, many missiles would have U.S. targets in their sights. And the CIA director suspected that the Soviet Luna rockets in Cuba were capable of greeting an invasion force with nuclear artillery shells, to a distance of twenty-five or thirty miles. "Invading is going to be a much more serious undertaking than most people realize," he told the president. "They had a hell of a lot of equipment before they got these things that you just saw pictures of. It's very evil stuff they've got there." Invasion "would be no cinch."[19]

At the UN Friday, Soviet and American diplomats gave notice that their governments would avoid confrontations at sea for at least a few days to see whether they could arrange a longer standstill with international oversight. Khrushchev told U Thant that he had ordered ships "not yet within the area of the American warships' piratical activities to stay out of the interception area, as you recommend." But the White House, fearing too much emphasis on events at sea, com-

---

[19] Detection of the Luna artillery weapons caused the Joint Chiefs to plan for comparable rockets in any American invasion force. But lacking evidence that the Lunas actually came with nuclear warheads, they never sought permission to include nuclear shells in the American contingency plan.

plained that it saw no sign of any Soviet intention to dismantle or stop work on the missile sites. So even as he scolded a State Department official for hinting at "further action," Kennedy gave Macmillan to understand that if diplomacy failed over the next forty-eight hours, "we are going to be faced with some hard decisions."

Khrushchev was meant to hear these private threats. And according to Sergei's reconstruction of events, the Soviet leader was in fact growing impatient with the pace of diplomacy. While the Presidium was listening to Gromyko reading the draft of another letter to Kennedy, which once again bitterly complained about the bases in Turkey, Khrushchev interrupted to lay bare his growing anxiety. As recalled by his son, he expressed these sentiments: *We have been warned that war could start today. Of course, it's possible the information was planted, but the risk is too great. America is gripped by a real frenzy and the military are thirsting for action. I therefore propose that we not involve U.S. missiles in Europe in the argument at this time. They're not bothering anyone. We have to concentrate on the main point: If the United States, their president, pledges not to attack Cuba, we will withdraw our missiles, despite the unpleasantness. Otherwise the situation becomes too dangerous.*

There is no record of what information caused Khrushchev to sound retreat. A prudent man needed not much more than Dobrynin's relay of the gossip at the press club bar—that "the president had supposedly taken a decision to invade Cuba" on Thursday or Friday night. That message lay atop Khrushchev's briefing folder Friday, along with the ambassador's "information that an order has been issued to bring the [U.S.] armed forces into maximum battle readiness." Also in that intelligence file was the news of Castro's order to shoot down American reconnaissance planes and General Pliyev's request, in view of rising tensions, to move his nuclear warheads closer to his missiles from their current location more than a hundred miles away.

Khrushchev brushed aside the proposed letter to Kennedy that Gromyko had drafted and instead dictated a long, highly emotional message of his own. It was full of complaints and accusations, claims of innocence and goodwill. Its climax, after twenty-five hundred words, was a fervent appeal for compromise and a promising but vague, even clumsy offer of a deal.

The raw copy of this letter, bearing the purple-ink signature and alterations by the chairman, reached the American embassy in Moscow before 10 AM Friday, Washington time (5 PM in Moscow). Duly translated, the text was delivered at about noon to the Central Telegraph on Gorky Street, but for reasons never explained, the letter languished there for more than six hours. The text only dribbled into the White House in segments, between 6 and 9 PM:

Dear Mr. President:

. . . From your letter, I got the feeling that you have some understanding of the situation which has developed and a sense of responsibility. I value this. . . .

You are mistaken if you think that any of our means on Cuba are offensive. However, let us not argue now. It is apparent that I will not be able to convince you of this. . . .

Why have we proceeded to assist Cuba with military and economic aid? The answer is: we have proceeded to do so only for reasons of humanitarianism. . . . We know how difficult it is to accomplish a revolution and how difficult it is to reconstruct a country on new foundations. . . .

You once said that the United States was not preparing an invasion. But you also declared that you sympathized with the Cuban counter-revolutionary emigrants, that you support them and would help them to realize their plans against the present Government of Cuba. . . .

If assurances were given by the President and the Government of the United States that the USA itself would not participate in an attack on Cuba and would restrain others from actions of this sort, if you would recall your fleet, this would immediately change everything. . . .

Let us therefore show statesmanlike wisdom. I propose: we, for our part, will declare that our ships, bound for Cuba, are not carrying any armaments. You would declare that the United States will not invade Cuba with its forces and will not support any sort of forces which might intend to carry out an invasion of Cuba. Then the necessity for the presence of our military specialists in Cuba would disappear. . . .

Mr. President, I appeal to you to weigh well what the aggressive, piratical actions, which you have declared the USA intends to carry out in international waters, would lead to. . . . If you did this as the first step towards the unleashing of war, well then, it is evident that nothing else is left to us but to accept this challenge of yours. If, however, you have not lost your self-control and sensibly conceive what this might lead to, then, Mr. President, we and you ought not now to pull on the ends of the rope in which you have tied the knot of war, because the more the two of us pull, the tighter that knot will be tied. . . .

Consequently, if there is no intention to tighten that knot and thereby to doom the world to the catastrophe of thermonuclear war, then let us not only relax the forces pulling on the ends of the rope, let us take measures to untie that knot. We are ready for this. . . .

Had it been promptly cabled to Washington, Khrushchev's intriguing proposal would surely have evoked a swift and positive response. Did the offer to withdraw "military specialists" mean all offensive *missiles*—a word that Khrushchev was still reluctant to commit to paper? Who would guarantee a total withdrawal? And who would guard against their return?

Such an exchange could have quickened the pace of peacemaking and greatly lightened the hours ahead. But reading Khrushchev's letter so late and in fragments, Kennedy decided to quit for the night, letting the analysts pore over the document and frame a thoughtful answer in the morning. With an endgame in sight, it never occurred to him that by dint of a twelve-hour delay the two nations would have to endure "Black Saturday," the bleakest day of the crisis.

NINE

NO VERY GOOD WAR

Wendy Hile Kennedy slept on Khrushchev's tantalizing suggestion—that if the United States promised not to invade Cuba then "the necessity for the presence of our military specialists in Cuba would disappear"—the Soviet leader found reasons to wish he could get his letter back. His diplomatic advisers complained that the proposal was so loosely drawn it might not be tempting enough to deter an American attack on Cuba. And his hawkish advisers complained that however useful to Castro, the proposed deal would bring the Soviets nothing except humiliation.

So Khrushchev reconvened his team and hurriedly composed another letter to Kennedy.

It was an elaboration on the text that Foreign Minister Gromyko had tried to offer the previous day, satisfying both of the new concerns. It called very clearly for the mutual withdrawal of missiles from Cuba and Turkey. And it specified that if the United States promised not to invade Cuba, the Soviet Union would promise never to invade Turkey. The Soviets knew that the Jupiters were obsolete, but in the eyes of the world, a mutual withdrawal would look more like a compromise, less like a Soviet defeat.

Khrushchev's second letter did not explain why he was amending the first proposal. But to make sure that the new proposition overtook the first, he ordered it broadcast by Moscow Radio late Saturday afternoon—the first public airing of any of the crisis letters.

It was still Saturday morning in Washington when news of the new Soviet proposal clicked on the White House teletypes. The initial reaction in ExCom was disbelief, a feeling that reporters were merely misreading the original Soviet proposition. When the full text arrived, doubt turned into dismay. It was a new and difficult proposal, all right, tying Cuba into a Turkey package. And compounding the difficulty was Khrushchev's odd decision to broadcast his demand to the entire world. That was sure to evoke a quick rejection by Turkey and perhaps other NATO allies.

The distress in ExCom was so great that Kennedy and his aides failed to savor some highly welcome words at the start of Khrushchev's proposition: "We agree to remove from Cuba those weapons which you regard as offensive." It was the first clear Soviet acceptance of the president's central demand.

Only then came the new Soviet price: "The United States, on its part, bearing in mind the anxiety and concern of the Soviet state, will evacuate its analogous weapons from Turkey."

Last but not least came the eminently acceptable idea for monitoring compliance with the deal: "Representatives of the UN Security Council could control, on the spot, the fulfillment of these commitments."

Khrushchev still could not bring himself to spit out the words *nuclear missiles*, but he left no doubt this time about what he was prepared to remove. His readiness to retreat should have thrilled the American crisis team. Yet compared with the vague and secret proposition that arrived Friday night, the new offer struck the group as downright devious. In Kennedy's view, a public withdrawal from Turkey was too painful to accept and yet too tempting to reject.

Khrushchev's letter went on to give assurances that there was time to safely complete all withdrawal arrangements. "The means situated in Cuba of which you speak and which disturb you, as you have stated, are in the hands of Soviet officers. Therefore, any accidental use of them to the detriment of the United States is excluded. . . . If there is no invasion of Cuba or attack on the Soviet Union or any of our other allies, then of course these means are not and will not be a threat to anyone."

All that, however, failed to solve the mystery of why he had sent two different propositions, which arrived only twelve hours apart. What could have happened in the Kremlin to produce the overlapping letters? Had the Russians finally caught up with the many unofficial suggestions of a Turkey swap—in *The Times* on Wednesday and in Walter Lippmann's column Thursday? Did endorsement of a swap by Chancellor Bruno Kreisky of Austria convince the Russians that they had somehow missed an offer from Kennedy?

If a Turkey-for-Cuba deal had been Khrushchev's first proposition, it might have found grudging acceptance in Washington. Kennedy felt from the start that he would much rather trade away an obsolete base in Turkey than Western rights in Berlin. But coming second, and under such strange and public circumstances, the same idea looked like a crude effort to raise the ante. Khrushchev's hectoring style still shone through the new letter, but it lacked much of the personal longing for peace that dominated the Friday message. Was he still in charge? Did hard-liners demote or depose him overnight? Was the first offer, without Turkey, still available? Or was all this confusion calculated to frustrate negotiations, to stall for time until more missiles were ready to fire?

The only Soviet guidance about the shift in Moscow came from Ambassador Zorin at the UN, who had been notoriously ill informed all week. He told U Thant that the confidential Khrushchev letter had been rushed off at a critical moment to relieve tension and prevent an attack but that the second letter was a more thought-through, substantive proposal.

In Washington, the fact that Moscow broadcast the second Khrushchev letter was seen as a clever stroke to inhibit Kennedy's options. As the president quickly realized, the Turks would refuse to become a bargaining chip in superpower poker, even if their Jupiters were immediately replaced by a superior Polaris submarine. The U.S. ambassador in Turkey, Raymond Hare, had explicitly warned that if withdrawal of the Jupiters became essential, it should be done *after* the Cuban crisis had passed and only through a *secret* understanding with the Russians.

The prevailing view in Washington was that the NATO alliance would be seriously damaged if the United States abandoned a European base merely to free itself from a threat that the French, British, Germans, and Italians had routinely endured. Yet as Kennedy observed, in grudging admiration of the Soviet move, the alliance would suffer an even greater shock if he rejected the deal and took action that provoked a counterattack in Europe. The allies would never forgive the United States for going to war after they learned that a deal for useless Jupiters had been available.

The president desperately wished that the Turks could still be persuaded to relinquish the Jupiters voluntarily. He complained bitterly that his diplomats had not prepared for this moment. Couldn't someone show the Turks that if the United States attacked Cuba, they would become a prime Soviet target? In his anger, the president came to believe, mistakenly, that he had long ago ordered the Jupiter bases closed. He had suggested it, but Turks considered the missiles on their soil to be a better guarantee of American support than an invisible submarine offshore. In any case, it was now too late to remove the Jupiters from the game. America's gain in Cuba seemed destined to incur pain in Europe.

Kennedy's only good riposte was to force Khrushchev back on the defensive, to complain that there was no point in bargaining so long as the Soviets continued the rapid construction of their missile bases. That work violated the pledges of restraint both nations had given to U Thant in recent days. So at midday Saturday, the White House issued a temporizing statement noting that it had received "several inconsistent and conflicting" proposals within twenty-four hours, including one that involved "the security of nations outside the Western hemisphere." Since the current crisis had been caused by a threat to the Americas, those other issues—meaning Turkey—would have to wait.

But the president refused to simply say no. He was haunted by the thought that he might be risking war in Cuba and Berlin and the unity of NATO for the sake of a few useless missiles in Turkey. Noting that it was past 8 PM in Moscow (noon in Washington), he asked the ExCom to adjourn for a few hours to devise a smarter reply with which to greet Khrushchev on his Sunday morning.

REMARKABLY, FIDEL CASTRO and his top commanders heard nothing on Saturday about either of Khrushchev's propositions. They received no copies of his letters to Kennedy and failed for some reason to pluck the public message off Moscow Radio. Nor were they told of the Kremlin's reaction to General Pliyev's request for permission to use "all available" antiaircraft weapons against an American aerial attack. Instead of answering that request, Marshal Malinovsky had fired off a two-sentence restraining order: "We categorically confirm that you are prohibited from using nuclear weapons from missiles, FKR [cruise missiles], 'Luna' [artillery rockets] and aircraft without orders from Moscow. Confirm receipt."

Khrushchev's readiness to withdraw his missiles from Cuba, therefore, came as a shock to Castro when he finally learned of it on Sunday. And the offer to sacrifice a Cuban interest for a Soviet benefit in Turkey deepened his dismay. But from Friday night until Sunday dawn, Fidel was diverted by fear of a U.S. attack and the excitement of preparing his defenses.

Castro's intelligence agents claimed to have learned late Friday that the United States was massing forces for an attack within seventy-two hours. These reports gained credence in Havana from the terrifying maneuvers of low-flying American fighter-bombers. As McNamara had boasted in ExCom, the Crusader planes were simulating attacks on the missile sites so that if they were ever ordered to destroy the Soviet bases they would have the benefit of surprise. But the simulations were all too real, with planes swooping down from three thousand feet to below five hundred.

So Castro assumed his favorite role, of military *commandante*. He ordered his antiaircraft gunners to fire at the low-altitude intruders. At the same time, he hectored the Soviet commanders of SAM units to track planes approaching at higher altitudes. And although the Soviet and Cuban forces were governed by separate national commands, their officers at many locations had bonded in enthusiastic support of a shared mission.

His martial adrenaline flowing, Castro decided to prepare Khrushchev for battle. He asked to huddle with Ambassador Alekseyev in the basement bunker of the Soviet embassy and dictated an emotional letter that the ambassador struggled until dawn to render into Russian. Fidel wrote that "aggression" was imminent, most likely an air attack limited to certain targets. Less probable, but possible, was an invasion, Castro added, in a passage whose meaning would be disputed for decades. An invasion, Fidel argued, would pose such a great threat to all humanity that the Soviet Union "must never allow" Americans to deliver the "first nuclear strike." Rather, it would be the moment for the Soviets "to eliminate such danger forever through an act of clear legitimate defense, however harsh and terrible the solution would be." The Cuban people were ready, Fidel promised, "to calmly confront a situation which we view as quite real and quite close."

Alekseyev sent a brief cable alerting Moscow to Castro's intimations of attack, but he did not send the whole dire message until later

Saturday morning, Havana time. Castro, meanwhile, went on the warpath. When the next wave of low-flying American planes roared over the island, he gave orders to chase them off with cannon fire. And his excitement aroused so much anxiety on the island's communications network that officers up and down the line were convinced that Cuba had been attacked or invaded.

What happened next has never been fully explained, even to Fidel Castro, but American scholars credit Russian and Cuban reports about the actions of two Soviet generals, both deputies of Pliyev. With Cubans shooting at American planes, the generals tried to find their commander for further orders. Unable to locate him, they decided they were obliged to help defend the island and so instructed their troops. And when the radar of a Soviet SAM battery in Banes, on the distant northeast coast of Cuba, locked on a U-2 flying at about seventy thousand feet—far beyond the range of Cuba's cannon—the Soviet unit was permitted to fire three SA-2 rockets, two of which knocked the spy plane from the sky.

Word of the kill spread quickly and was widely celebrated by the Cubans. When reported to Moscow, it drew a modest rebuke from Marshal Malinovsky, who deplored the attack as interference with an already promising diplomacy to resolve the crisis. Khrushchev and Kennedy, however, feared not just for their diplomacy. Both sensed that they were losing control over their military forces.

FOR EXCOM ON SATURDAY, there was no end of the bad news. First came word that an entirely different U-2, based in Alaska, had strayed for forty-five minutes over Soviet territory near the Chukotsk Peninsula, while sampling the air for nuclear-test fallout. Soviet fighter planes scrambled to intercept the intruder, but so did an American F-102, which managed to guide the lost pilot back out to sea.

Soon after, McNamara reported a U-2 overdue from Cuba. And then came his report that one of the low-flying Crusader (RF-8A) reconnaissance planes had returned after being struck by a twenty-millimeter shell. When he confirmed that the missing U-2 had been spotted on the ground and that the pilot, Major Rudolf Anderson Jr., lay dead inside, there seemed good reason for Kennedy's plaintive query, "Well now, this is much of an escalation by them, isn't it?"

Cuban guns had struck the Crusader, but the Kennedy team assumed that they were fired with Soviet consent or collaboration. And if the high-flying U-2 was shot out of the sky, as the president assumed, that was surely the work of a Soviet SAM. Had not Khrushchev sent assurances, that very morning, that he had full command of all Soviet weapons? The inevitable, albeit wrong inference in ExCom was that Khrushchev had decided to knock out American reconnaissance so that he could rearrange and complete the missile deployment.

Castro's new militancy found an echo among Kennedy aides. At the very least, General Taylor now wanted permission to act on Kennedy's prior resolve to destroy SAM units that fired at American planes.

And McNamara momentarily lost all cool. "The military plan now is very clear," he said. "A limited strike is out. We can't go on a limited strike without the reconnaissance aircraft. So the military plan now is basically invasion, because we've set a large strike to lead to invasion." There might still be time later to cancel the invasion, he added, but "we should start the strike, call up the reserves." He also wanted to avert a counterattack on Turkey by notifying the Russians that a Polaris submarine in the Mediterranean would replace the Jupiters. Not until Rusk observed that this would shift the risk of countermeasures to Berlin did McNamara back off.

The secretary's confusion was all too typical of the responses to the tumble of bad news. It was left to Thompson to point out that sending a Polaris sub to replace the Jupiters would actually achieve a Soviet objective without getting anything in return. Thompson kept nudging the president back toward accepting Khrushchev's first proposition—a no-invasion pledge for a Soviet withdrawal from Cuba, with the European issues shoved aside for negotiation at a later time. Thompson also proposed offering the no-invasion pledge in public, to reclaim a propaganda advantage.

The idea of thus answering only the first, vague Friday offer, while ignoring the second explicit proposition of Saturday, has been admired erroneously as a "Trollope ploy," after the habit of the novelist's heroines to take the smallest sign, like the squeezing of a hand, as a proposal of marriage. Kennedy did seize upon the hint of a deal in Letter No. 1 but he by no means ignored the proposal in Letter No. 2.

The president deliberately refused to evade the Jupiter issue so completely that Khrushchev could accuse him of rejecting it. If the crisis ultimately led to war and the Russians grabbed Berlin, he remarked, everyone would say, " 'Well, that [Turkey deal] was a pretty good proposition.' " The president felt trapped. Now that Khrushchev had made the Turkey proposal in public, he would have to accept it.

Not necessarily, Thompson persisted. Since Khrushchev maintained that all the trouble began with American threats against Cuba, he might want above all to boast that he had removed the invasion threat. McCone quickly saw the point: "The important thing for Khrushchev, it seems to me, is to be able to say, 'I saved Cuba. I stopped an invasion.' " Robert Kennedy concurred. But McNamara wanted the next message to include a demand that they stop shooting at his aircraft.

As various officials struggled Saturday afternoon to devise a reply to Khrushchev, the Joint Chiefs recommended a major air strike no later than Monday. Vice President Johnson, a relatively modest contributor to the week's discussion thus far, favored getting tough in two directions at once—tough with the Turks if they blocked a crisis-ending agreement and tough on any SAM sites that were shooting at American planes. Thompson reiterated that Khrushchev's "almost incoherent" letter of Friday showed him to be so worried he would probably remain open to his original proposal, without the Turkey swap.

Yet Kennedy kept looking at himself through the eyes of others—foreigners who marveled at his Cuba obsession, allies who did not want to sacrifice Berlin for a modest American gain, Americans who might lose loved ones just to keep obsolete missiles in Turkey. "We can't very well invade Cuba with all the toil and blood it's going to be," the president declared, "when we could have gotten them out by making a deal on the same missiles in Turkey. If that's part of the record, then I don't see how we'll have a very good war."

BY 7 PM (3 AM SUNDAY IN MOSCOW), Robert Kennedy and Sorensen had finally polished a delicately balanced message to Khrushchev. It accepted the no-invasion pledge that the Soviet leader had seemed to suggest in his Friday night letter—as Thompson urged. But it also made brief reference to the second letter, as the president thought necessary. Kennedy said he was ready to end the quarantine and to promise not to invade Cuba if the Soviets withdrew offensive weapons under UN supervision. Then, he continued, with world tensions reduced, he would be ready to address a "more general arrangement regarding 'other armaments,' as proposed in your second letter." Above all, however, the work in Cuba had to stop. If the missile threat persisted and European issues were used to prolong the discussion, the risk to peace would be "grave."

With the crisis nearing a climax, Kennedy decided not to rely only on these diplomatic hints and feints. He decided to give Khrushchev a more explicit incentive to settle and a more graphic threat if he refused. The written message, like Khrushchev's latest, was broadcast immediately, over the Voice of America. But the president also asked brother Bobby to deliver a copy to Ambassador Dobrynin together with a secret oral message for the chairman.

To shape this supersecret message, the president drew seven men into the Oval Office, out of range of the hidden microphones—Rusk, Ball, and Thompson from State, McNamara and Gilpatric from Defense, Bundy and Sorensen from the White House staff. And it was Secretary of State Rusk, though always maligned by the Kennedy clan for his lack of creativity, who best understood the president's desire. He drew on the sage advice of his ambassador in Turkey and gave the Kennedy brothers a lesson in the power of devious diplomacy. He proposed giving Khrushchev a Turkey IOU.

As Dobrynin reported to the Kremlin, he was summoned Saturday night to the office of a "very upset" Robert Kennedy. But this time, he observed, the attorney general "didn't even try to get into fights on various subjects, as he usually does, and only persistently returned to one topic: time is of the essence and we shouldn't miss the chance."

Robert Kennedy's account of the meeting agreed. "I told him first that we understood that the work was continuing on the Soviet missile bases in Cuba. Further, I explained to him that in the last two hours we had found that our planes flying over Cuba had been fired upon and that one of our U-2s had been shot down and the pilot killed. I said these men were flying unarmed planes. I told him that this was an extremely serious turn in events. We would have to make certain decisions within the next 12 or possibly 24 hours. There was very little time left. If the Cubans were shooting at our planes, then we were going to shoot back."

Robert Kennedy said he needed a commitment—by Sunday—that the bases would be removed. He was careful to add, unconvincingly, that this was not an "ultimatum," just a "statement of fact." There were generals, and not only generals, "itching for a fight." If war broke out, millions of Americans as well as Russians might die. But if work on the bases stopped and they were then removed, the United States would, as requested, promise not to allow or participate in an invasion of Cuba.

And what about Turkey? Dobrynin asked.

Whereupon Bobby delivered Rusk's astutely framed IOU: If Turkey turned out to be the only obstacle to a deal, the president saw no "insurmountable difficulties" in resolving the issue. But the Soviets needed to understand that the Turkey bases were created by NATO, and the United States could not unilaterally abandon them or even publicly discuss their removal under Soviet threat. "We need 4 to 5 months" to close them down, and they would be closed down in that time—provided the Soviet leaders respected the U.S. promise as a secret, never to be linked with the Cuban missile deal.

Dobrynin's relay of this message was direct and accurate. Bobby's own memo for the files, addressed to Rusk, was drafted truthfully, but then edited to deceive posterity, through the deletion of one sentence. As left in State Department files, the memo said Bobby had firmly refused to consider the Jupiters in Turkey as part of any Cuba deal. But the copy left in Kennedy's files showed that before it was typed, Bobby had penciled out a sentence that truthfully conveyed a contrary meaning: "If some time elapsed—and per your [Rusk's] instructions, I mentioned four or five months—I said I was sure that these matters could be resolved satisfactor[il]y."

Rusk had grown so worried about the subtlety of his Turkey maneuver that he telephoned Robert Kennedy to make certain he delivered it as "information, not a public pledge." As Rusk wrote in his memoir, "Bobby told me that he was then sitting with Dobrynin and had already talked with him. Bobby later told me that Dobrynin called this secret message 'very important information.' "[20]

In even deeper secrecy, the president and Rusk then plotted a still

---

[20] It seems certain that this is the phone call that Dobrynin, many years later, wrongly recalled as having occurred on Friday rather than Saturday and described, also erroneously, as a call from Bobby to the president. Until he confessed the error, Dobrynin thus gave rise to speculation that the Kennedy brothers had directly urged the ambassador to pursue the Turkey swap *before* Khrushchev's proposal of it.

more circuitous diplomatic escape route.[21] If Khrushchev persisted in demanding a *public* U.S. commitment to remove the Jupiters, they wanted to prepare a way to give such a promise without seeming to yield to a Soviet demand. Rusk suggested a way to make a Jupiter deal look like the proposal of United Nations diplomats. He drafted a statement that proposed a Turkey–Cuba swap and telephoned the text to Andrew Cordier, then president of Columbia University, a former UN official and friend of both Rusk and Secretary-General Thant. On further signal from Rusk, Cordier was to prompt U Thant to issue this statement, opening the way for Kennedy to accept from the secretary-general what he did not want to accept directly from Khrushchev.

AT NINE O'CLOCK SATURDAY NIGHT, the ExCom reconvened to apply additional psychological pressures on Khrushchev. One was a McNamara press conference to announce that unarmed American planes had been fired upon, to describe surveillance of Cuba as essential, and to warn that future photo flights would have fighter escorts. Equally unsubtle was McNamara's call-up of twenty-four troop carrier squadrons of the air force reserve for potential use in an invasion. In another telephone conversation with Scotty Reston, which I overheard, Kennedy subtly added to the public pessimism. The president described his puzzlement over the two Khrushchev messages, revealed the loss of a U-2 to what he presumed to have been hostile fire, and portrayed a generally worsening situation for *The Times*'s Sunday edition.

Yet behind the scenes, the Kennedy brothers stoutly continued to resist suggestions to rush toward military action. The president wanted to let the next Cuba-bound tanker, the *Grozny*, carrying missile fuel tanks as well as oil, pass unmolested; it would be enough, he said, to ask U Thant to remind Khrushchev of his pledge to halt such traffic. If more action was needed, Kennedy indicated, he planned on

---

[21] Not revealed, by Rusk to James Blight, until twenty-five years later!

Sunday to add petroleum products to the embargo list, announce his intention to stop *all* Soviet shipping to Cuba, and activate twenty-nine private ships as troop carriers to enliven speculation about an invasion.

And if his reconnaissance planes drew more fire on Sunday, the president said he planned to threaten air attacks against *all* the Soviet bases, but not before Tuesday. Although he did not tell the full ExCom about his brother's secret Jupiter offer to Dobrynin or about the preparation of a public Turkey deal through U Thant, Kennedy obviously intended to give diplomacy more time.

Still another opportunity for tough talk—and delay—presented itself in Europe. Kennedy had already summoned the NATO Council so that his representative could explain the risks of Soviet retaliation in Europe in case the United States were to attack Cuba. But now that the Jupiter missiles were in play, the president did not want anything involving Turkey to be debated among the allies. He therefore asked that the council meeting be turned into a superficial "briefing" of the Europeans, combined with somber warnings, sure to be heard by Moscow, that the situation was "deteriorating."

Kennedy's long face alarmed many of his colleagues and even historians reading the record in later years. But it must have hidden a touch of relief in his heart. He still had no good explanation for the two overlapping Khrushchev letters or for the burst of antiaircraft fire in Cuba. But even assuming the worst, such as a hard-liner revolt in the Kremlin, the most recent message from Moscow had been an unambiguous offer to meet his central demand that the missiles be removed—and for a price that he knew, in the end, he was ready to pay.

WHILE MANY OFFICIALS PREPARED to spend a tense night in their offices, Kennedy called for Dave Powers, his court jester, to sit with him through a favorite movie. It was *Roman Holiday*, William Wyler's charming romance about a princess, Audrey Hepburn, who manages for twenty-four hours to escape burdensome royal inhibitions for a fling around Rome with an American reporter, Gregory Peck. Paradoxically, the tale, Cinderella in reverse, won an Oscar for the then unacknowledged author, Dalton Trumbo, who had been blacklisted for refusing to testify about his membership (1943–1948) in the Communist party and his alleged sympathies for the Soviet Union.

No less incongruous was the jazz band performing at the same hour aboard an American destroyer at the quarantine line in the Caribbean. It was entertaining the crew of a Soviet submarine forty yards away.

The Soviet sub, called B-59, was one of four originally sent to open a base for nuclear submarines at the Cuban port of Mariel but later reassigned to escort duty for cargo ships. Each of those subs carried a dozen torpedoes, including one that was nuclear-tipped and kept under special round-the-clock guard. Unaware of this nuclear touch, the U.S. Navy relished the chance to practice its antisubmarine tactics, dropping "practice depth charges" the size of hand grenades to try to force the Soviets to surface. As one Soviet officer recalled, the explosions felt as if a sledgehammer was beating against a metal barrel. The frightened crew of B-59, already faint from heat, exhaustion, and malnutrition after a month at sea, finally had to reach for air to recharge the sub's batteries. Flying a large Soviet flag, the vessel bobbed to the surface, surrounded by the aircraft carrier *Randolph* and half a dozen American destroyers.

What ship? asked the destroyer *Cony.*

Ship X, replied the angry sub.

What is your status?

On the surface, operating normally.

Do you need assistance?

No, thank you.[22]

---

[22] These details were obtained from Soviet records and interviews by Peter A. Huchthausen, who served aboard the destroyer *Blandy* during the crisis, and are recounted in his *October Fury*. Hoboken, NJ: John Wiley & Sons, 2002.

After a navy plane further harassed the sub by dropping incendiary devices to illuminate the scene for its official cameras, the *Cony* softened and signaled an apology. And after a while, the Soviet captain allowed his signalmen to ask one of the destroyers for bread and cigarettes. The Americans shot a line across the water and sent the supplies. And then, in the morning's first light, the Soviet crew heard frolic aboard several American ships and observed a jazz band on the aft deck of one destroyer. It featured "a tall black man wearing a tall baker's hat" on trombone. He was playing "Yankee Doodle."

TEN

ALL OF THEM?

NIKITA KHRUSHCHEV SHOULD HAVE SLEPT WELL SATURDAY
night. He had found a way to disguise his retreat—as a gain for
both Cuba and the Soviet Union on terms that he already knew
Kennedy could accept. After all, the idea of a Turkey-for-Cuba deal
had figured prominently all week in leaks from Washington, and a
no-invasion promise had been offered by Kennedy himself in conversation with Gromyko the week before. But the night brought new
perils, and the Soviet leader awoke Sunday morning to fearful alarms.

Castro's prediction of imminent attack arrived before dawn.
Khrushchev blanched as he heard Fidel's proposal that he should not
let the United States strike "the first nuclear blow." That message
could only mean that Castro favored a preemptive, all-out nuclear attack on the United States, igniting a global conflagration. Whether or
not he noticed Castro's qualifier—*if Cuba is invaded*—Khrushchev
thought his client had gone mad.[23]

---

[23] In a posthumous sequel to his memoirs, *Khrushchev Remembers: The Glasnost*

Also overnight came the KGB's account of John Scali's improvised warning that an invasion of Cuba was only "hours away." The ABC correspondent had felt betrayed when his brokerage of a no-invasion deal was overtaken by Khrushchev's formal proposal of a Turkey–Cuba swap. So he angrily and loosely predicted war to Alexander Fomin, his Soviet embassy contact.

Then, in midmorning, Marshal Malinovsky revealed to Khrushchev that a U-2 had been shot down in Cuba, killing the American pilot—a report cast in such a way as to lead Khrushchev to believe, for many years after, that the Cubans were to blame.

Whoever was to blame, by noon on Sunday events seemed to be spinning out of control. Khrushchev summoned his Presidium to the government's suburban dacha and sounded a final retreat.

The anxious meeting in Moscow focused first on Kennedy's public message, which agreed to give Cuba a no-invasion pledge but made no direct mention of Turkey. The discussion was soon interrupted, however, by a telephone call from Gromyko, who reported a "quite alarming" telegram from Dobrynin. The ambassador had met Saturday night with a "very upset" Robert Kennedy, who demanded an urgent Soviet response. He was said to have promised, off the record, that the Jupiters would be removed from Turkey in four or five months. This could not, however, be revealed as part of the deal.

<hr />

Tapes (Schecter, Jerrold L., ed. and translator, with Vyacheslav V. Luchkov. Boston: Little, Brown, 1990), the Soviet leader asserts that Castro had urged him to order an immediate nuclear attack against the United States. As a denial that same year, Castro published a Spanish text of his October 28, 1962, letter to the Soviet leader, in which he conditioned his "first blow" proposal on a U.S. invasion, calling it less likely than an air attack, but possible. By way of explanation in 1990, Castro said an invasion would have been met with nuclear artillery and he had meant only to embolden Khrushchev in that event not to wait for the United States to strike the first nuclear blow against the Soviet Union—as Stalin had foolishly waited for the Nazis to invade in 1941. The Russian text of Castro's letter, as Khrushchev read it in 1962, has not been published.

And unless agreement was reached by Sunday, an attack on Cuba might be unavoidable.

Running this message through his preconceptions about the United States, Khrushchev concluded that the Pentagon was gaining the upper hand and that there was even danger in Washington of a military coup. The Cuban drama had become so acutely personal that both Kennedy and Khrushchev came to fear at critical moments that the other might be overthrown.

And then came word that the president would deliver a major television address at 5 PM Moscow time (9 AM in Washington). The Presidium felt a dread moment at hand. In just a few hours, Kennedy would declare war, launch an attack against Cuba, and challenge Soviet forces far from home to a battle they could not win.

Wasting no more time, Khrushchev dictated a strikingly warm letter of surrender:

> Esteemed Mr. President:
>
> I express my satisfaction and gratitude for the sense of proportion and understanding you have shown of the responsibility borne by you at present for the preservation of peace throughout the world. . . .
>
> The Soviet government, in addition to previously issued instructions on the cessation of further work at building sites for the weapons, has issued a new order to dismantle the weapons which you describe as "offensive" and to crate and return them to the Soviet Union. . . .
>
> The Soviet government decided to help Cuba with means of defense against aggression—and only with means for purposes of defense. We stationed defense means there which you call offensive. . . .
>
> I regard with respect and trust your statement . . . that there will be no attack, no invasion of Cuba—not only by the United States but also by other nations of the Western Hemisphere. . . .

In lengthy asides, the Soviet leader bemoaned Kennedy's hostility toward the Castro regime. He also complained about intrusions into Soviet and Cuban airspace, especially by the U-2 over Chukotsk Peninsula, which, he said, could have easily been mistaken for a nuclear bomber. Back to business, he then agreed to let United Nations inspectors verify the dismantling of his Cuban bases and designated Vasily Kuznetsov, a first deputy foreign minister, to handle negotiations in New York. Implicitly accepting Robert Kennedy's demand for secrecy, the chairman made no mention of the promise that the Jupiter missiles would be withdrawn from Turkey in four or five months.

Even before this message was completed, Gromyko cabled Dobrynin to "quickly get in touch with R. Kennedy" and tell him that a "most favorable" response would be read over Moscow Radio shortly. Typically, this alert reached the ambassador ninety minutes *after* the broadcast of Khrushchev's letter, which suffered its own dizzy delay.

Although the Communist party's chief propagandist, Leonid Ilyichev, had volunteered to personally carry the Khrushchev script to Radio Central, his chauffeur got lost on the half-hour drive into town. When Ilyichev finally reached the studio, Sergei Khrushchev recalled, his elevator got stuck between floors and the fateful message had to be passed through the cage's grille, one page at a time.

After listening to the broadcast of his letter, Khrushchev again led the Presidium in a display of solidarity and calm. They went over to the Kremlin Theater, where a visiting Bulgarian repertory company performed a play called *At the Foot of Vitosha*—a mountain peak not far from the seaside resort at which Khrushchev always claimed to have made the decision to plant his missiles in Cuba.

THE KENNEDY SPEECH that the Soviet leaders feared might be a declaration of war turned out to be merely a rebroadcast of the president's crisis declaration of the previous Monday. So the extra haste in

Moscow, although excessive, brought Washington a euphoric Sunday morning.

The president received the news of Khrushchev's readiness to withdraw a few minutes after nine, in the same bedroom where thirteen days earlier he had first learned of the missile deployment. His relief and elation were hard to contain.

An equally cheerful Robert Kennedy received Dobrynin in midmorning. He again warned the ambassador that the promise concerning the Jupiters in Turkey had to remain a shared secret. The reason for secrecy was respect for the NATO allies, but it had the effect of exaggerating Khrushchev's defeat and Kennedy's victory. In their ignorance of the Turkey swap, journalists and even some ExCom members were already celebrating a total American triumph, claiming that Khrushchev had yielded entirely to American demands.

Only the Joint Chiefs felt defeated. They thought they smelled a Soviet trick and proposed an attack the next morning unless there was "irrefutable evidence" of the dismantling. General Taylor relayed that message to the president, but he registered his personal dissent. His colleagues seemed to have lost all perspective.

Kennedy went to church, then met with the ExCom to hear Rusk courteously praise the contributions of both hawks and doves, because both military threats *and* diplomacy had contributed to a satisfying resolution. Bundy, having turned hawk at the end, knew better; he praised the doves for keeping diplomacy at the fore, but he did so without identifying the president as the leading dove in the room.[24]

---

[24] The terms *hawk* and *dove* gained currency in the Cuban Missile Crisis and were popularized soon after in an inflammatory article in *The Saturday Evening Post* by Stewart Alsop and Charles Bartlett, the latter a close friend of the president. It accused Adlai Stevenson of advocating "a Munich" in the Caribbean by proposing to offer withdrawal from bases in Turkey and Italy and perhaps also from Guantánamo. The president's defense of Stevenson was lukewarm, perhaps to disguise his own, similarly dovish approach to the crisis and perhaps also to avenge Stevenson's reluctance to endorse Kennedy in 1960.

McNamara crisply returned to business. He saw no need for further confrontations at sea. He said American C-130s, painted white, stood ready to serve UN inspectors of the missile withdrawals. And since Khrushchev had promised to pull out "the weapons which you describe as 'offensive' "—without once mentioning "missiles"—the president was persuaded to demand the withdrawal also of the IL-28 bombers.

Kennedy begged his colleagues not to gloat about victory. He urged them to emphasize the difficulties of inspecting the withdrawal, the survival of a communist regime in Cuba, the likelihood of further trouble in Berlin, the dangers of subversion throughout Latin America. But the group's denials of victory that day were delivered with a wink. There was no disguising the jubilation that pervaded the commentaries in print and on Sunday television programs, despite all White House exhortations.

David Schoenbrun of CBS told Richard Reeves that he was called in midbroadcast by the president's press secretary, Pierre Salinger, and urged to avoid talking about a Soviet "defeat." He was told that Khrushchev could be so humiliated and angered that he would change his mind. More likely, however, Kennedy feared that the Soviet leader would feel compelled, in despair, to betray the Jupiter secret, to boast that he had after all achieved a comparable American retreat, from Turkey.

At noon on Sunday, Kennedy broadcast a statement that welcomed Khrushchev's willingness to take "reciprocal" measures. He told the American people that while much remained to be negotiated, the crisis was over. By evening, the president sent a respectful message to Khrushchev that left the quarantine in place until the agreements were carried out. He explained, but without apology, the U-2 intrusion over Chukotsk. And he expressed a hope for more agreements "as we step back from danger," particularly in the field of arms control.

The president's real mood was betrayed in his jest to Bobby, which alluded to Lincoln's assassination at Ford's Theatre after he had prevailed in the Civil War. "This is the night I should go to the theater," Kennedy said.

WHILE HIS ADVERSARIES IN WASHINGTON struggled to protect Khrushchev from humiliation, his comrades in Havana exploded with rage. And the Cubans, even more than the Turks, had good reason to feel trampled in the superpowers' rush out of crisis.

Fidel received the news of Soviet withdrawal through an AP dispatch, read to him by his journalist friend, Carlos Franqui. Castro shouted "Son of a bitch! Bastard! Asshole!" Franqui recalled. "Fidel went on in that vein for quite some time. The Russians had abandoned us, made a deal with the Americans and never even bothered to inform us. Fidel had no idea. He went on cursing, beating even his own record for curses."

General Pliyev confirmed his orders to withdraw when Castro visited Soviet headquarters in Cuba. After a lengthy silence, Fidel asked, "All of them?"

"All."

In what President Dorticós called a "volcanic" temper, Castro refused to see his friend, the Soviet ambassador, for four days. Only after the whole world learned of Moscow's decision to recall the missiles did the Cuban leader receive a direct communication from Khrushchev. And instead of soothing the Cuban's wounds, Khrushchev lectured him against freelance military action. In fact, Khrushchev accused Castro of having made matters worse by shooting down the American U-2.

"I would like to recommend to you now, at this moment of change in the crisis, not to be carried away by emotion," Khrushchev wrote. Yes, the United States violated international law. But now that the crisis is being settled—"in your favor"—the Pentagon will be looking to frustrate the agreement. "Therefore I would like to advise you in a friendly manner to show patience, firmness and even more firmness" and to avoid "provocations."

Castro fumed that the deal was struck behind his back, on terms that left him at the mercy of American power. He compared Cuba's plight to that of Czechoslovakia, when it was abandoned to Hitler's mercy by the Western powers on the eve of World War II. He looked on approvingly as Cuban university students chanted, "*Nikita, mariquita, lo que se da, no se quita.*" Nikita, you faggot, what's been given should not be taken away.

Publicly, Castro denounced the no-invasion pledge as worthless, a hedged promise by a relentlessly hostile neighbor. If Khrushchev had wanted to achieve security for Cuba, he should have demanded an end of the trade embargo, an end to all subversion against the Castro regime, an end of aerial intrusions, and an American withdrawal from Guantánamo. In a cold private letter, Castro stiffly told Khrushchev to go and read Cuba's public statements to learn what he thought of the final accord. He told the Soviet leader to ask his own commanders for a more accurate account of the fate of the downed U-2. And while he agreed to stop shooting at American reconnaissance planes, it would be "only for as long as the negotiations last."

As for Khrushchev's cavalier offer to let United Nations observers witness the dismantling of the missiles in Cuba: "I also wish to inform you," Castro added, "that we are in principle opposed to an inspection of our territory." More colorfully, he told associates that anyone coming to inspect Cuba had better come dressed in battle armor.

The Chinese communists were delighted to dig into Castro's wounds with their own tales of Soviet betrayal. They mocked the missile deployment as "adventurism" and the withdrawal as "capitulationism."

By comparison, Kennedy managed Turkey's humiliation with superb sleights of hand. First thing Monday morning, the State Department accepted with straight face the Turkish ambassador's "gratitude" that the Jupiters were *not* traded away in any deal with Moscow. On that very day, Defense Secretary McNamara ordered secret preparations to close down the Jupiter bases by April 1—the five-month deadline promised to Khrushchev.

On Monday also, Khrushchev tried to assure himself some credit for the Turkey deal with a secret letter recording the commitment of the Kennedy brothers. It emphasized that all his terms for ending the crisis "took into account the fact that you had agreed to resolve the matter of your missile bases in Turkey." But Bobby returned that letter to Dobrynin on Tuesday as unacceptable. The promise would be kept and it could be discussed with a small number of knowing officials, he said, but there must be no hint of the deal in any document. "Very privately," Dobrynin remembered, "Robert Kennedy added that some day—who knows?—he might run for president, and his prospects could be damaged if this secret deal about the missiles in Turkey were to come out."

"Father was not offended" by this rebuff, Sergei recalled. The chairman just kept up his feverish letter-writing to salvage something from his Cuban debacle. In four thousand rambling words, Khrushchev pleaded with Kennedy to give him a few things with which to assuage Castro. Why not call off the quarantine without further delay? And with the crisis over, why not end the American trade embargo? Why the "laughable" claim that the obsolete IL-28 bombers posed an "offensive" threat and must also leave Cuba? And wouldn't it be a boon to peace if the United States liquidated the base at Guantánamo, which "is only a burden for your budget"? Maybe they could then agree to abandon all military bases everywhere, and all military alliances as well, and settle the last little questions about which flag should fly over West Berlin. And if China were allowed into the United Nations, they could take up complete and general disarmament! The pie was flying in the sky.

Equally disingenuous was the two-thousand-word message to Castro in which Khrushchev said he heard that "some Cubans" were unhappy with his withdrawal, even though it had prevented a war in which millions of people would have died. Khrushchev said he also

heard "there are opinions" that he had failed to consult about the settlement when in fact "we consulted with you, dear Comrade Fidel
Castro." Recalling Cuba's warning to him of an imminent American
attack, Khrushchev asked, "Wasn't this consultation?" Most directly,
Khrushchev complained about Castro's willingness to suggest a nuclear first strike by the Soviet Union. He did not doubt that Cubans
were ready to die heroically, but "we are not struggling against imperialism in order to die." The aggressor was preparing to attack Cuba
"but we stopped him." So "we view this as a great victory."

Castro replied by deploring the "misinterpretation" or mistransla-
tion of his words. He said he never begged for the removal of the Soviet missiles even though he knew Cuba would be annihilated in a
nuclear war. He just meant, and still believed, that if the United States
had attacked Cuba, Russians would also come under attack, and that
would be the time not to let the United States strike the first nuclear
blow. As for consultation, not just a few Cubans but many "are expe-
riencing at this moment unspeakable bitterness and sadness" and
"more than ever need to trust in themselves."

With clever and cogent arguments, Castro resisted U Thant's personal plea to admit UN observers to the missile bases. Even Cuban
soldiers had been barred from those bases, he countered. Besides, if
the UN trusted the American promise not to invade Cuba, why not
trust the Soviet promise to withdraw the missiles? In any case, if
Cuba's friends had to withdraw their weapons from the island, why
not require Cuba's enemies to do likewise? At least give us back
Guantánamo!

Cuba's resistance left Soviet and American diplomats scrambling
to devise an alternate inspection routine. Khrushchev sent Mikoyan
rushing back to Havana even as his wife of forty years lay dying in the
Kremlin hospital. But Castro was not easily moved. He also balked at
having observers at the loading docks. Soviet and American negotia-
tors finally arranged to have the departing freighters carry the missiles as deck cargo and uncover them at sea, where they could be

photographed by American planes and helicopters. The last of the missiles were reported withdrawn by November 11, but in a way that further damaged Khrushchev's standing with his military. Decades later, recalling the departures, General Gribkov said that "in the 54 years that I have served as a military man—my most humiliating experience was the inspection of our ships at sea."

Ten more days were needed to pay Kennedy his last ounce of tribute: removal of the old IL-28 bombers that Castro wanted to keep as a gift, and which the Americans had in fact tolerated when they first arrived. The Pentagon had more reason to fear the MiG-21 fighter planes that were being left behind, but the president was squeezing full advantage from Khrushchev's coy pledge to "dismantle the weapons which you describe as 'offensive.'" Mikoyan passed up his wife's funeral and struggled for three weeks to overcome Castro's resistance while Kennedy and Khrushchev exchanged multiple letters that slowly narrowed the disagreements.

Finally on November 20, Khrushchev had Castro's consent to promise removal of the IL-28s within a month, whereupon Kennedy formally lifted the quarantine. The Cubans tried for three more days to hold on to some of the tactical nuclear rockets, but Mikoyan, again delaying his departure, insisted that their withdrawal was required by laws mandating strict Soviet control over nuclear weapons.

In a final sop to Castro, the Soviets left a three-thousand-man combat brigade on the island so that any attack would acquire global significance. American intelligence, having badly misjudged the size of the Soviet force to begin with, overlooked this remnant. The Carter administration was shocked to discover that a brigade still served in Cuba—seventeen years later!

Kennedy took full advantage of Khrushchev's quarrels with Castro, whom he intended to keep harassing with covert actions and economic boycott. Since Castro refused to admit UN inspectors, the president refused to formally deliver his no-invasion pledge to the world organization. He merely asserted at a press conference that he would "neither initiate nor permit aggression in this hemisphere" so long as offensive weapons were kept out "under adequate verification." For the time being, that verification would be accomplished by American reconnaissance planes, whose flights were not to be interfered with.

Unable to boast of any reciprocal concession in Turkey, Khrushchev spent the winter of 1962–1963 desperately arguing that his missile adventure had succeeded, as intended, in preventing the overthrow of the Castro regime. Defending Cuba, he insisted, had always been his motive in sending the missiles. But Castro's failure to show any gratitude undermined the claim, as did the Cuban leader's displays of growing sympathy for Khrushchev's rivals in Communist China. Not the least of Khrushchev's losses was the discredit brought upon his claim of many years that he possessed such effective long-range nuclear missiles on Soviet territory that he did not "need" missile bases abroad.

In the final days of 1962, Khrushchev suffered one more moment of torment when Kennedy greeted the 1,113 survivors of the Bay of Pigs invasion whom he had ransomed from Castro for fifty-three million dollars worth of medical supplies and baby food. Presented with the banner of Brigade 2506 in Miami's Orange Bowl, the president responded with guilty passion, and without benefit of script, that "I can assure you that this flag will be returned to this brigade in a free Havana."

TO LURE CASTRO BACK into the Soviet fold, Khrushchev had to rely mainly on charm and economic aid. In late January, he composed one of the more remarkable diplomatic documents of his era—an avuncular, almost paternal seven-thousand-word letter to Fidel begging for his understanding and visit. It began with a wish that Castro could see the lovely Russian forests, silvery with frost. And it expressed a yearning "to see you and to talk, to talk with our hearts open."

Still, the underlying theme was bitter. Whereas he had faced danger and forced the United States to choose between an invasion of Cuba and a thermonuclear war, Khrushchev wrote, "certain socialist states" are not only misrepresenting the Soviet actions but shouting Marxist slogans to disguise the fact that they did nothing to help Cuba when it faced "mortal danger." So much for China. Obviously envisioning Kennedy's reelection and service until 1968, the chairman claimed to have secured at least six years of peace for Castro. He begged him to use the time to develop his economy, because "it is this revolutionary example of Cuba's that the North American monopolists and imperialists most fear." Finally, recognizing Castro as a "southern man" who enjoyed warm weather, he urged him to visit Moscow in the spring, to join the May Day celebrations and to accompany Khrushchev on hunting and fishing trips.

Castro went for a month, landing in the Soviet Union on the very day that the last Jupiters came out of Turkey. Their withdrawal was represented to the world as an upgrading of NATO weaponry, the replacement of vulnerable bases with an invulnerable missile-firing Polaris submarine cruising the Mediterranean. When he was asked by a Senate committee to give assurances that the withdrawal of Jupiters was "in no way, shape or form, directly or indirectly connected with the settlement, the discussion or the manipulation of the Cuban situation," Secretary Rusk, like McNamara in other settings, simply lied. "That is correct, sir," he answered. And though the lie was widely disbelieved—as the question made clear—it was not reliably exposed for more than a decade.

Khrushchev was not so lucky with his dissembling. The old man lavished affection on his young Cuban visitor and seemed to be making progress with the advice that Cuba's economic development take precedence over revolutionary politics in Latin America. In a rare treat, Castro was shown a Soviet intercontinental missile on its launch pad, which he asked to inscribe with his name. "If it is used, God forbid," he said, "let the U.S. imperialists know that it's a greeting from

Cuba." But the tour was spoiled at Khrushchev's hunting lodge one night as he read aloud from the file of his secret exchanges with Kennedy. The chairman carelessly included excerpts from a letter in which the president spoke of having fulfilled his "commitments" to pull Jupiters out of Turkey and Italy.

"When this was read," Castro recalled decades later, "I looked at him and said, 'Nikita, would you please read that part again about the missiles in Turkey and Italy?' He laughed that mischievous laugh of his. He laughed, but that was it. I was sure that they were not going to repeat it again because it was like that old phrase about bringing up the issue of the noose in the home of the man who was hung."

Ever so casually, Khrushchev had exposed the flaw in his claim that the whole crisis had been run for Cuba's sake and benefit. Then again, Castro was well rewarded for his forgiveness. All the SAM missiles in Cuba were granted him as a gift, provided only that he not fire them at unarmed U-2 reconnaissance planes. And Castro left Moscow assured that he would never again have to pay anything for the continuing supply of Soviet weaponry.

WITH WHAT CASTRO SHREWDLY perceived to be Kennedy's new, crisis-honed authority, both at home and abroad,[25] the president reached out to Khrushchev in mid-1963 to try to redefine their Cold War relationship. In an address at American University on June 10, which the Soviet leader found extremely moving, the president paid tribute to Soviet sacrifices and achievements and proposed that they build a genuine peace—"the kind of peace that makes life on earth

---

[25] In the November 6 voting, the Democrats won twenty-five of thirty-nine contested Senate seats, a net gain of four, and remarkably, in a nonpresidential election, lost only four seats in the House, retaining a comfortable majority.

worth living, the kind that enables men and nations to grow and to hope and to build a better life for their children."

The immediate fruit of this new spirit was a hot-line teletype connection to permit instant communication during a crisis, without reliance on Western Union bicyclists or public broadcasts. In addition, negotiations were begun to facilitate the sale to the Soviet Union of large amounts of subsidized American wheat. And a few swift strokes completed an agreement to end all nuclear testing in the atmosphere—leaving only underground tests, which the United States refused to limit without inspections of Soviet territory.

Overnight, the issue of Berlin, which Kennedy always considered to lie at the heart of the Cuban crisis, simply evaporated. There were no more ultimatums to chase the West out of the city and no more threats to let East Germans control Western access to Berlin. When Dean Rusk visited Khrushchev at his Black Sea home after signing the test-ban treaty in August 1963, they played a vigorous game of badminton prior to what the secretary remembered as a blood-chilling Berlin finale.

Khrushchev raised a question that had obviously tormented him for many years. "Mr. Rusk," he asked, with only his interpreter present, "[Chancellor] Konrad Adenauer has told me that Germany will not fight a nuclear war over Berlin; [President] Charles de Gaulle has told me that France will not fight a nuclear war over Berlin; [Prime Minister] Harold Macmillan has told me that England will not fight a nuclear war over Berlin. Why should I believe that you Americans would fight a nuclear war over Berlin?"

Quite a question, Rusk remembered.

"With Khrushchev staring at me with his little pig eyes, I couldn't call Kennedy and ask, 'What do I tell the son of a bitch now?' So I stared back at him and said, 'Mr. Chairman, you will have to take into account the possibility that we Americans are just goddamn fools.'

"We glared at each other, unblinking, and then he changed the subject and gave me three gold watches to take home to my children."

ELEVEN

HOW FAR THE BRINK

THE CRISIS PASSED, BUT ITS SHADOW LINGERED FOR decades and its lessons, some real, some imagined, loom over us still.

Just one year after he proclaimed the end of the affair, in November 1963, President Kennedy was shot dead in Dallas by a demented drifter who had tried to enlist as a defender of the Cuban revolution. Lee Harvey Oswald had spent three years in the Soviet Union, attempting to sell himself as an anti-American hero, but he was recognized as a chronic, psychotic misfit and sent back to the United States.

Oswald fired the fatal shots on the very day that Jean Daniel, a French journalist, met with Castro in Havana to convey what he thought had been Kennedy's secret encouragement to explore the chances of improving relations between the United States and Cuba. Castro wanted to break Kennedy's trade embargo, but he had no intention of being lured out of the communist camp. For a time, he even taunted the Russians by siding ideologically with the Chinese. It was not until the Soviet Union reduced its aid in the 1980s and finally collapsed in 1991, in Castro's fourth decade as Cuba's dictator, that Fidel tried to turn a more benign face toward the United States.

The Kennedy assassination killed more than a dynamic young president at the peak of his popularity. It also removed a leader who had stared down a Soviet challenge and begun, with his enhanced stature and reputation for toughness, to seek a new, more stable relationship with the Russians. Paradoxically, because his triumph over Khrushchev was achieved with restraint and even respect, Kennedy had gained Khrushchev's confidence and hoped to realize the live-and-let-live accords that he failed to sell in their only meeting in Vienna.

Kennedy's closest aides, and also some historians, have mourned the loss of an equally great opportunity to avert the war in Vietnam. They contend that Kennedy's success in the Missile Crisis would have allowed him, even emboldened him once reelected, to let South Vietnam fall to communist control without committing Americans to a calamitous jungle war.

I do not agree with that judgment, which is in any case highly speculative. One could argue with equal weight that the Missile Crisis helped stimulate American intervention in Vietnam. The crisis left the ExCom members who survived their president dangerously over-confident about their ability to "manage" foreign crises. At the heart of the Vietnam tactics that McNamara, Rusk, and Bundy urged upon Lyndon Johnson lay the arrogant conviction that civilians in Washington could manipulate military operations and escalating threats to achieve political and diplomatic goals, as they had done in the Missile Crisis. But it is true that President Johnson, for all his brilliance in legislative politics, lacked Kennedy's subtle appreciation of foreign affairs and the protective armor that Kennedy acquired in the Missile Crisis for seeking compromises with communist governments.

In any event, the postcrisis history of the Soviet Union was as fluid as our own, with domestic imperatives, as always, driving foreign policy. Despite his face-saving tokens of a no-invasion pledge and Jupiter withdrawal, Khrushchev's claims of victory in the Missile Crisis rang hollow around the world. He suffered a huge loss of diplomatic prestige and military credibility. Among Soviet elites, he could no longer hide the Soviet Union's strategic inferiority, and his military leaders would have balked at negotiated deals to limit their weapons development. As Vasily Kuznetsov remarked when he reached the United Nations to negotiate the end of crisis, "Well, Mr. McCloy, you got away with it this time, but you will never get away with it again." True to his forecast, the Soviets pursued nuclear parity with the United States and essentially achieved it, at great cost, around 1970.

Khrushchev had continued to believe that two to three hundred long-range missiles were enough to deter a U.S. nuclear attack, and he tried in the spring of 1963 to reassert his desire to cut military budgets to serve civilian needs. His ultimate objective, according to Sergei, was to reduce the Soviet army to half a million men backed by a national militia with reserve officers trained in college programs. He pressed these opinions on his generals in dogmatic, even insulting ways, adding to their sense of humiliation in the Missile Crisis and depriving him of their support when his civilian associates conspired in 1964 to remove him from power.

Many factors drove this conspiracy. Foremost among them were Khrushchev's failure to realize his rash forecasts of economic success, his latest scheme for promoting efficiency by curtailing the power of senior Communist party officials, and his alienation of the military. The Presidium members also resented his increasingly quarrelsome and arbitrary methods, his bluster, his scapegoating and rule by fiat. They were alarmed by the growing hostility of Communist China and listed the Cuban venture as an example of Khrushchev's "harebrained scheming."

In mid-October 1964, precisely two years after Americans stumbled upon the first missile launchers in Cuba, the seventy-year-old Khrushchev was summoned from his Black Sea villa and forced to resign—for reasons of "advanced age and deteriorating health." He was replaced by an oligarchy led by Leonid Brezhnev, who repaid the military leaders for their support with a massive military buildup, propelling an arms race with the United States that drained the resources of both nations and contributed mightily to the economic collapse and political ruin of the Soviet Union.

There is no way to imagine the course of world events if Kennedy and Khrushchev had survived in office and been allowed to explore a less hostile relationship. The passions and suspicions produced by two decades of Cold War were not easily overcome. And successive leaders in Moscow and Washington had to grapple with tensions until the end of the century. But the two governments fully absorbed the lesson that war between the superpowers had become unprofitable and that they were obliged to prevent peripheral issues from ever again creating a comparable risk of a military clash.

HOW GREAT, THEN, WAS THE RISK? How near did we come to the brink of the abyss that Kennedy and Khrushchev evoked in their correspondence and surely dreaded in the darkest hours of the crisis?

"That this was the most dangerous crisis of the nuclear age," McGeorge Bundy wrote, "does not tell us how dangerous it was." Neither does the worldwide anxiety produced by the massing of hostile forces in the Caribbean and the hurling of muscular threats accompanied by ominous military alerts. Even the calmest officials inside the Kremlin and White House, who knew their side had no taste for war, could not be sure the feeling was fully reciprocated in the rival capital. Kennedy and Khrushchev, it turns out, were equally determined to avoid even a minor clash out of fear that it would trigger an uncontrollable escalation of violence. But they could not be sure of the adversary's restraint until the end of the crisis, which gave them daily reasons to fear that mindless subordinates or dumb accidents could stampede them into battle.

The truth, with the benefit of hindsight, is that two responsible and highly intelligent men were firmly in charge of both governments and they were determined to avoid a war, certainly a nuclear war. They understood throughout that no issues of national survival were at stake and they suspected, correctly, that powerful domestic pressures more than aggressive foreign ambition had led them into confrontation. Long after the crisis, Khrushchev praised the president as levelheaded—"he didn't let himself become frightened but also didn't let himself become intoxicated by the might of the United States." And Kennedy, according to his brother, "believed from the start that the Soviet Premier was a rational, intelligent man."

Paradoxically, however, Khrushchev and Kennedy deemed it useful after the crisis to exaggerate the danger they had surmounted. The chairman had to justify his retreat by arguing desperately that his settling for a face-saving deal had saved the world from nuclear devastation. The president, on the other hand, needed to redefine himself as bold in the face of grave danger, no longer the weak and vacillating leader of his first Cuban venture. So Khrushchev encouraged the view that "the world was on the brink of thermonuclear catastrophe in those days" and Robert Kennedy wrote in a self-serving recounting of the crisis about a world brought "to the abyss of nuclear destruction and the end of mankind."

Over the decades, journalists, memoirists, scholars, and screenwriters gladly exploited such hyperbole, practicing a literary brinkmanship about the nearness of the brink to enhance the drama of their renderings of the affair. Probably the most melodramatic expressions have come from Robert McNamara, whose grief for his subsequent role in Vietnam has since made him question the risks run over Cuba as well. He argued in 1998 that the "world came within a hair breadth of nuclear war" and that "we lucked out"—an opinion that contradicted his more accurate recollection that Kennedy still had many ways to "tighten the screws" of the blockade and was never close to ordering an invasion.

I hope I have demonstrated that Khrushchev, like Kennedy, was determined to avoid even a non-nuclear clash. His refusal to consider a counterblockade in Berlin was proof enough that he dared not risk a conflict even where he enjoyed some tactical advantage. Nor did he threaten to attack America's bases in neighboring Turkey, though he clearly equated the Jupiters with his missiles in Cuba. The moment Kennedy challenged the Soviet deployment, Khrushchev recalled the seven missile-firing submarines that he was hoping to base in Cuba, realizing they were in no sense "defensive" and therefore provocative. He refused to fire at American reconnaissance planes even after they had uncovered his secret deployment. He accelerated the negotiations when he thought the Cubans were becoming hard to restrain. He reinforced the orders against the use of nuclear weapons even if Cuba were invaded. And although his personal prestige and political future were heavily invested in the Cuban venture, Khrushchev never strayed from his private assertions—to Dobrynin and others—that war against the United States had to be avoided at all costs.

And as shown by some of the closest students of the crisis—James G. Blight and Philip Brenner[26]—"Kennedy was both more flexible than the early postmortems suggested and more sensitive to the Soviet need to salvage something positive from the crisis." In the equally thorough finding of Professor John L. Gaddis, Kennedy pushed for compromise more strongly than anyone else in his administration: "Far from placing the nation and the world at risk to protect his own reputation for toughness, [Kennedy] probably would have backed down, in public if necessary, whatever the domestic political damage might have been."[27]

Having decided to do more than protest to compel Khrushchev to withdraw the missiles, Kennedy chose a blockade, which was the least provocative available measure. In fact, he chose the least provocative kind of blockade—a "quarantine" aimed only at "offensive weapon

---

[26] Blight, James G. and Philip Brenner. *Sad and Luminous Days: Cuba's Struggle with the Superpowers After the Missile Crisis.* New York: Rowman & Littlefield, 2002.

[27] Gaddis, John Lewis. *We Now Know: Rethinking Cold War History.* New York: Clarendon Press, 1997.

equipment"—which left him the option of later adding petroleum products or a full economic blockade against Cuba. As he said in his first speech of the crisis, Kennedy was prepared to endure "months" of tension before he realized his objective. Moreover, the president delayed any real enforcement of the quarantine to gain time for negotiation; when he finally felt a need to make a show of enforcement, he chose to board a non-Soviet ship whose cooperation had been carefully orchestrated. And if finally forced to challenge a Soviet vessel that was determined to run the blockade, Kennedy envisioned merely crippling its rudder and towing it to port, taking care to avoid casualties. Even after Major Anderson's U-2 was shot down on the last Saturday, Kennedy rescinded his prior commitment to retaliate immediately against the offending Soviet SAM battery. And in the concluding negotiations, he not only agreed in secret to eventually vacate the Jupiter bases in Turkey but also stood ready, if necessary, to sacrifice NATO interests by doing so in public.

Both Kennedy and Khrushchev chose to ride roughshod over weak allies in Cuba and Turkey to settle the conflict. Kennedy's main concern on that worrisome last Saturday was that Khrushchev had decided for some reason to prevent all further American reconnaissance over Cuba. But even then, his indicated answer would have been a public warning that the Russians had fired first and thus invited retaliation against their SAM sites—a clash that Khrushchev had already shown himself unwilling to risk. And if an attack became necessary and led Khrushchev to strike back at the Jupiters in Turkey, Kennedy gave orders to absorb the blow without further escalation. If all else failed, he intended to tighten the blockade, still avoiding an invasion that would have engaged Russians and Americans in ground combat.

Of course, as the two leaders were the first to fear, accidents happen. They both fretted about the U-2's accidental intrusion into Soviet territory, and Kennedy was most uneasy about the navy's use of "practice" depth charges against Soviet submarines as well as the random acts of sabotage by Cuban exiles infiltrated under Operation Mongoose. But risks of Soviet–American conflict had arisen often before during the Cold War, and they were usually defused. American planes had often strayed over Soviet terrain. Soviet subs had often roamed annoyingly through American waters. Soviet and American ships had "bumped" at sea and their planes had "buzzed" rival ships. Tanks had maneuvered menacingly at the wall in Berlin, and assorted stratagems had been used periodically to harass American traffic to Berlin. Indeed, ground transport to Berlin had been completely blocked in 1948, a time of unquestioned American military superiority, but the West's answer was a nonviolent airlift of supplies rather than a frontal challenge.

From the Soviet side we have the testimony of Andrei Gromyko, the stolid foreign minister who knew Khrushchev's purposes as well as anyone and who is said to have expressed reservations about the missile deployment when first proposed. He remarked years later that throughout the Cold War, "today, yesterday, the day before yesterday," there had always been a certain degree of risk. But in the Missile Crisis, "a direct threat of nuclear war did not exist. . . . I say these words—I ask you to believe that I say them—with good reason."

Sergei Khrushchev said his father believed that as long as events were controlled by the two heads of government, "the threat of war was practically nonexistent." But as a man who had lived through two wars and knew what could happen in situations when troops were tense, and located very close to one another, his father also knew that "an unexpected decision, an unexpected shot, for example, could lead to loss of control over events."

That control required the assertion of command over the top military men, in full awareness that they are by nature devoted to action and contemptuous of diplomacy. Khrushchev and Kennedy had learned from bitter experience to exert that control. And as they improvised their way through the crisis, they never wavered in their understanding that neither nation's vital interests were threatened in the

Cuban affair. There was no reason for either of them to risk the huge casualties of a nuclear exchange. Even if by inadvertence, miscalculation, or accident the two powers had resorted to violence, both leaders had ample reasons, already articulated to themselves, to reverse course. They were determined to avoid the brink.

By temperament and predicament, Khrushchev and Kennedy produced the Cuban Missile Crisis. By temperament and predicament, they brought it prudently under control. Luck played a role in their quick appreciation of the danger and in their swift agreement to back away. But it was not dumb luck.

ACKNOWLEDGMENTS

There is no adequate way to relate how much I have learned about diplomatic history, and about the Missile Crisis in particular, from the hundreds of government officials, scholars, and journalists whom I have encountered over the past half century. And for that unending education, I am deeply indebted to the four families that have shaped my life: my own, and those constituting the owners, the staffs, and the readers of *The New York Times*. Priceless kinships all.

This book's greatest immediate debt is owed to Joyce Purnick, my wife, colleague, and editor-in-chief. It would not have been written without her selfless encouragement; once written, it benefited immeasurably from her love, her penetrating eye, and her strategic advice.

Invaluable as well have been the scholarship and writings credited in the bibliography, and most especially those cited in the introductory author's note.

The idea for another look at the Missile Crisis came from my most helpful editor at Ballantine Books, Zachary Schisgal. He was prompted in turn by an article I wrote for *Smithsonian*, commissioned by its editor, Carey Winfrey. I have profited also from the close readings of the manuscript by my agent, Jane Gelfman, and my daughter Margot.

Elisabeth Dyssegaard next became my enthusiastic editor and booster and also provided the efficient assistance of Signe Pike. The conscientious copy editing of Laura Jorstad, a freelancer engaged by Josh Karpf of Ballantine Books, saved me from several embarrassments. The elegant design of this book is by Casey Hampton, commissioned by Ballantine's Dana Blanchette.

Like many writers before me, I have been blessed by the research resources available at the New York Public Library. And I had the privilege there of a desk in the Frederick Lewis Allen Memorial Room, which treats writers as honored guests. My special thanks to that facility's considerate gatekeeper, Wayne J. Furman of the special collections staff.

The search for relevant photographs and permissions to reproduce them leaves me indebted to friends and colleagues at *The New York Times:* Arthur O. Sulzberger Jr., chairman and publisher; Thomas K. Carley, president of news services; Nancy Lee, vice president for business development in news services; Jim Mones, director of archives; Phyllis Collazo, photo sales representative; and Dennis Laurie, morgue supervisor. Also to James Hill and Maryrose Grossman of the Audiovisual Archives of the John F. Kennedy Library; Bill Creighton of United Press International; and Nell Whiting of *Smithsonian.*

For unearthing a cheerful photo of the author, the credit belongs to *The Times*'s indefatigable Bill Cunningham.

ILLUSTRATION

ACKNOWLEDGMENTS

1. Neal Boenzi, *The New York Times*.
2. The John F. Kennedy Library.
3. United Press International.
4–5. The John F. Kennedy Library.
6. *The New York Times*.
7–8. *The New York Times*, from the John F. Kennedy Library.
9. United Press International.
10–14. White House photos by Cecil Stoughton, from the John F. Kennedy Library.
15. *The New York Times*.
16. Neal Boenzi, *The New York Times*.
17. White House photo by Robert Knudsen, from the John F. Kennedy Library.
18. United Press International.

BIBLIOGRAPHY

The Presidential Recordings: John F. Kennedy. General editors: Philip Zelikow and Ernest May. New York: W. W. Norton, 2001.

- Naftali, Timothy, ed. *The Great Crises, Volume One: July 30–August 1962.*
- Naftali, Timothy and Philip Zelikow, eds. *The Great Crises, Volume Two: September–October 21, 1962.*
- Zelikow, Philip, and Ernest May, eds. *The Great Crises, Volume Three: October 22–28, 1962.*

Abel, Elie. *The Missile Crisis.* New York: J. P. Lippincott, 1966.

Allison, Graham T. *Essence of Decision: Explaining the Cuban Missile Crisis.* Boston: Little, Brown, 1971.

Allison, Graham T., and Philip Zelikow. *Essence of Decision: Explaining the Cuban Missile Crisis,* 2nd ed. New York: Longman, 1999.

Allyn, Bruce J., James G. Blight, and David A. Welch. *Back to the Brink: Proceedings of the Moscow Conference on the Cuban Missile Crisis, January 27–28,*

1989. Cambridge, MA: Center for Science and International Affairs, Harvard University, 1992.

Ball, George W. *The Past Has Another Pattern*. New York: W. W. Norton, 1982.

Beschloss, Michael R. *The Crisis Years*. New York: HarperCollins, 1991.

Blight, James G., Bruce J. Allyn, and David A. Welch. *Cuba on the Brink: Castro, the Missile Crisis and the Soviet Collapse*. New York: Pantheon, 1993.

Blight, James G., and Philip Brenner. *Sad and Luminous Days: Cuba's Struggle with the Superpowers After the Missile Crisis*. New York: Rowman & Littlefield, 2002.

Blight, James G., and David A. Welch, eds. *Intelligence and the Cuban Missile Crisis*. Portland, OR: Frank Cass, 1988.

Blight, James G., and David A. Welch. *On the Brink: Americans and Soviets Reexamine the Cuban Missile Crisis*. New York: Noonday Press, 1990.

Brinkley, Douglas. *Dean Acheson: The Cold War Years, 1953–1971*. New Haven, CT: Yale University Press, 1992.

Brugioni, Dino A. *Eyeball to Eyeball: The Inside Story of the Cuban Missile Crisis*. Robert F. McCort, ed. New York: Random House, 1991.

Brune, Lester H. *The Cuba-Caribbean Missile Crisis of October, 1962*. Claremont, CA: Regina Books, 1996.

Bundy, McGeorge. *Danger and Survival: Choices About the Bomb in the First Fifty Years*. New York: Random House, 1988.

Burlatsky, Fedor. *Khrushchev and the First Russian Spring*. Translated by Daphne Skillen. London: Weidenfeld and Nicolson, 1991.

Chang, Laurence. *The Cuban Missile Crisis, 1962*. New York: New Press, 1992.

Chang, Laurence, and Peter Kornbluh, eds. *The Cuban Missile Crisis, 1962: A National Security Archive Documents Reader*. New York: New Press, 1998.

Clifford, Clark, with Richard Holbrooke. *Counsel to the President*. New York: Random House, 1991.

The Cuban Missile Crisis: A Briefing Paper. Avalon Project at Yale Law School. http://elsinore.cis.yale.edu/lawweb/avalon.

Cuban Missile Crisis and Aftermath. Foreign Relations of the United States, 1961–1963. Volume XI. Washington: Department of State.

Dallek, Robert. *An Unfinished Life: John F. Kennedy 1917–1963*. Boston: Little, Brown, 2003.

Detzer, David, *The Brink: Cuban Missile Crisis, 1962*. New York: Thomas Y. Crowell, 1979.

Dinerstein, Herbert S. *The Making of a Missile Crisis: October, 1962*. Baltimore: Johns Hopkins University Press, 1976.

Dobrynin, Anatoly. *In Confidence: Moscow's Ambassador to America's Six Cold War Presidents (1962–1986)*. New York: Times Books, 1995.

Eubank, Keith. *The Missile Crisis in Cuba*. Malabar, FL: Krieger Publishing, 2000.

Franqui, Carlos. *Family Portrait with Fidel: A Memoir*. Translated by Alfred MacAdam. New York: Random House, 1984.

Fursenko, Aleksandr, and Timothy Naftali. *"One Hell of a Gamble": The Secret History of the Cuban Missile Crisis—Khrushchev, Castro and Kennedy, 1958–1964*. New York: W. W. Norton, 1997.

Gaddis, John Lewis. *We Now Know: Rethinking Cold War History*. New York: Clarendon Press, 1997.

Garthoff, Raymond L. *Reflections on the Cuban Missile Crisis*, rev. ed. Washington: Brookings Institution, 1989.

Gribkov, General Anatoli, and General William Y. Smith. *Operation Anadyr: U.S. and Soviet Generals Recount the Cuban Missile Crisis*. Chicago: edition q, 1994.

Hershberg, James G. "New Evidence on the Cuban Missile Crisis: More Documents from the Russian Archives." Cold War International History Project Bulletin 8-9, winter 1996–1997.

Hilsman, Roger. *The Cuban Missile Crisis*. Westport, CT: Praeger, 1996.

Huchthausen, Peter A. *October Fury*. Hoboken, NJ: John Wiley & Sons, 2002.

Kennedy, Robert F. *Thirteen Days: A Memoir of the Cuban Missile Crisis*. New York: W. W. Norton, 1969.

Khrushchev, Sergei N. "The Military-Industrial Complex, 1953–1964." In *Nikita Khrushchev*. William Taubman, Sergei Khrushchev, and Abbott Gleason, eds. New Haven, CT: Yale University Press, 2000.

———. *Nikita Khrushchev and the Creation of a Superpower*. Translated by Shirley Benson. University Park, PA: Penn State University Press, 2000.

Koenker, Diane P., and Ronald D. Bachman, eds. *Revelations from the Russian Archives: Documents in English Translation*. Washington: Superintendent of Documents, 1997.

Kramer, Mark. "Tactical Nuclear Weapons, Soviet Command Authority, and The Cuban Missile Crisis." Cold War International History Project—Virtual Archive. http://wwics.si.edu/index.

Lechuga, Carlos. *In the Eye of the Storm: Castro, Khrushchev, Kennedy and the Missile Crisis.* Melbourne: Ocean Press, 1995.

May, Ernest, and Philip Zelikow. *The Kennedy Tapes: Inside the White House During the Cuban Missile Crisis.* Cambridge, MA: Belknap Press, 1997.

McAuliff, Mary S. *CIA Documents on the Cuban Missile Crisis, 1962.* New York: W. W. Norton, 1969.

Medland, William J. *The Cuban Missile Crisis of 1962: Needless or Necessary?* New York: Praeger, 1988.

Nash, Philip. *The Other Missiles of October: Eisenhower, Kennedy and the Jupiters, 1957–1963.* Chapel Hill: University of North Carolina Press, 1997.

Nathan, James A. *Anatomy of the Cuban Missile Crisis.* Westport, CT: Greenwood Press, 2001.

Nathan, James A., ed. *The Cuban Missile Crisis Revisited.* New York: St. Martin's Press, 1992.

The New York Times, October 15–31, 1962.

O'Donnell, Kenneth P., and David F. Powers, with Joe McCarthy. *"Johnny, We Hardly Knew Ye": Memories of John Fitzgerald Kennedy.* New York: Pocket Books, 1973.

Pious, Richard M. "The Cuban Missile Crisis and the Limits of Crisis Management." *Political Science Quarterly,* spring 2001.

Pope, Ronald R., ed. *Soviet Views on the Cuban Missile Crisis: Myth and Reality in Foreign Policy Analysis.* Washington: University Press of America, 1982.

Ranelagh, John. *The Agency: The Rise and Decline of the CIA.* London: Weidenfeld and Nicolson, 1986.

Reeves, Richard. *President Kennedy: Profile of Power.* New York: Simon & Schuster, 1993.

Rusk, Dean, as told to Richard Rusk. *As I Saw It.* Daniel S. Papp, ed. New York: W. W. Norton, 1990.

Salinger, Pierre. *John F. Kennedy Commander in Chief: A Profile in Leadership.* New York: Penguin Putnam, 1997.

Schecter, Jerrold L., ed. and translator, with Vyacheslav V. Luchkov. *Khrushchev Remembers: The Glasnost Tapes.* Boston: Little, Brown, 1990.

Schlesinger, Arthur M. Jr. "Four Days with Fidel: A Havana Diary." *New York Review of Books,* March 26, 1992.

———. *A Thousand Days: John F. Kennedy in the White House.* Boston: Houghton Mifflin, 1965.

Shakhnazarov, Georgi. "Fidel Castro, Glasnost, and the Caribbean Crisis." Cold War International History Project—Virtual Archive. http://wwics.si.edu/index.

Shapley, Deborah. *Promise and Power: The Life and Times of Robert McNamara.* Boston: Little, Brown, 1994.

Sorensen, Theodore C. *Kennedy.* New York: Bantam, 1966.

Stern, Sheldon M. *Averting 'The Final Failure': John F. Kennedy and the Secret Cuban Missile Crisis Meetings.* Nuclear Age Series. Stanford University Press, 2003.

Szulc, Tad. *Fidel: A Critical Portrait.* New York: William Morrow, 1986.

Talbott, Strobe, ed. and translator. *Khrushchev Remembers: The Last Testament.* Boston: Little, Brown, 1974.

Tatu, Michel. *Power in the Kremlin: From Khrushchev to Kosygin.* New York: Viking, 1969.

Taubman, Philip. *Secret Empire: Eisenhower, the CIA, and the Hidden Story of America's Space Espionage.* New York: Simon & Schuster, 2003.

Taubman, William. *Khrushchev: The Man and His Era.* New York: W. W. Norton, 2003.

Thompson, Robert S. *The Missiles of October.* New York: Simon & Schuster, 1992.

Troyanovsky, Oleg. "The Making of Soviet Foreign Policy." In *Nikita Khrushchev.* William Taubman, Sergei Khrushchev, and Abbott Gleason, eds. New Haven, CT: Yale University Press, 2000.

Weisbrot, Robert. *Maximum Danger: Kennedy, the Missiles, and the Crisis of American Confidence.* Chicago: Ivan R. Dee, 2001.

White, Mark J. *The Cuban Missile Crisis.* New York: Macmillan, 1996.

———. *Missiles in Cuba: Kennedy, Khrushchev, Castro and the 1962 Crisis.* Chicago: Ivan R. Dee, 1997.

Wise, David, and Thomas B. Ross. *The U-2 Affair.* New York: Random House, 1962.

Zubok, Vladislav. "The Case of Divided Germany, 1953–1964." In *Nikita Khrushchev.* William Taubman, Sergei Khrushchev, and Abbott Gleason, eds. New Haven, CT: Yale University Press, 2000.

INDEX

ABOUT THE AUTHOR

MAX FRANKEL is one of America's preeminent journalists. He worked for *The New York Times* for fifty years, rising from college correspondent to reporter, Washington bureau chief, editorial page editor, and ultimately executive editor from 1986 to 1994. He won the Pulitzer Prize for his coverage of President Nixon's trip to China in 1972. He wrote the nationally bestselling memoir *The Times of My Life and My Life with the Times*. He lives in New York City.